Plebiscites and Sovereignty

About the Book and Author

Throughout the world, civil wars, secessionist struggles, wars of national liberation, and irredentist movements are producing casualties and refugees at a staggering rate. In an environment of international turmoil, traditional modes of inter-state diplomacy are often ineffective when political legitimacy and sovereignty, self-determination and territorial integrity are in conflict. Dr. Farley argues that although largely ignored in times of unfettered state sovereignty, the plebiscite is an increasingly effective tool of conflict resolution in an age of militant popular sovereignty. Dr. Farley identifies the circumstances and conditions under which a plebiscite can resolve sovereignty crises, discusses the practical process of conducting an internationally supervised election, and analyzes the roles that neutral states, international organizations, and outside observers play in providing expertise and resources for the conduct of plebiscites.

Lawrence T. Farley is associate professor of political science at Lock Haven University and author of *Change Processes in International Organizations* (1982).

Plebiscites and Sovereignty

The Crisis of Political Illegitimacy

Lawrence T. Farley

Westview Press • Boulder
Mansell Publishing Limited • London, England

This volume is included in Westview's Special Studies in International Relations.

This softcover edition was manufactured at Westview Press using equipment and methods that allow us to keep even specialized books in stock. It is printed on acid-free paper and bound in softcovers that carry the highest rating of the National Association of State Textbook Administrators, in consultation with the Association of American Publishers and the Book Manufacturers' Institute.

Published in 1986 in the United States of America by Westview Press, Inc.; Frederick A. Praeger, Publisher; 5500 Central Avenue, Boulder, Colorado 80301

Published in 1986 in Great Britain by Mansell Publishing Limited, 6 All Saints Street, London N1 9RL

Library of Congress Cataloging-in-Publication Data
Farley, Lawrence T., 1947-
Plebiscites and sovereignty.
(Westview special studies in international relations)
Bibliography: p.
Includes index.
1. Plebiscite. 2. Self-determination, National.
I. Title. II. Series.
JX4054.F37 1986 321'.05 85-31520
ISBN 0-8133-7217-8

British Library Cataloguing in Publication Data
Farley, Lawrence T.
Plebiscites and sovereignty: the crisis of political illegitimacy.
1. Plebiscite.
I. Title.
327.1'72 JX4054
ISBN 0-7201-1832-8

Composition for this book was provided by the author.
This book was produced without formal editing by the publishers.

Printed and bound in the United States of America

The paper used in this publication meets the minimum requirements of the American National Standard for Permanence of Paper for Printed Library Materials Z39.48-1984.

6 5 4 3 2 1

Contents

Preface

The techniques of war have received the foremost attention of mankind throughout history. Our bookshelves groan under the weight of books detailing the strategy and tactics of warfare. Works that focus upon peace are proportionally few in number and many of them depict simply the horrors of war. Studies of the practical techniques of making peace are pitifully few in number. Indeed, mankind's collection of peacemaking techniques is uncomfortably small:

balance of power
deterrence
negotiation
good offices
mediation and conciliation
arbitration
adjudication
plebiscite

Clearly, our kit of peacemaking instruments is small--some of the instruments rusty from lack of use. While they are not formidable, they are all that mankind has at this the most heavily armed period of human history. The plebiscite is but one of these techniques--yet it is fundamentally different from the others. The other methods are based upon the state-centric view of international relations where states--not individual human beings--are the only recognized participants in international affairs. The sovereign--originally a monarch and now typically an elective government--has the indisputable right to acquire and dispose of land and people. Thus, most techniques of peacemaking are founded on the assumption that peace is made between sovereign states--not between peoples.

The most important political trend of the past millenium has been the persistent, worldwide increase in the level of political participation. This trend has transformed the substance of civic life in every corner of the planet. The "will of the people" has become the bedrock of political legitimacy in the domestic politics of nearly every state. Yet this notion of "popular sovereignty" seems to have had little impact upon the conduct of international relations. States remain the almost exclusive units of international intercourse. Land and people may be bartered by governments without seeking the consent of those whose livelihoods and national identities are at stake.

In the twentieth century a serious challenge has begun to emerge to the principle of unfettered state sovereignty. This challenge, the doctrine of "national self-determination," is simply an expression at the international level of the millenial trend toward greater popular participation in civic life.

If there is one future trend that can be forecast with great confidence it is that demands for greater popular participation in international diplomacy will increase--especially in cases where land and people are on the negotiating table.

Hence, the plebiscite--an ignored and abused orphan in the age of state sovereignty--would seem destined to become an essential tool of diplomacy in the approaching age of increased popular sovereignty. From a cynical device used by eighteenth and nineteenth century conquerors to ratify their conquests, the plebiscite has developed into a sensitive tool of conflict resolution. The plebiscites conducted following World War One and the plebiscites carried out by the United Nations Trusteeship Council since World War Two illustrate the essential usefulness of the technique.

David Fromkin reminds us that:

> The world since 1945 has been at war almost continuously, even though the citizens of the prosperous countries have been sufficiently unaffected to be able to pretend that they have been living in a world at peace. Warfare has been adapted to the requirement of today's world.

The techniques of peacemaking must also be adapted to the requirements of today's world. The twenty-eight "small" wars currently (the mid-1980s) in progress are creating casualties and refugees at a rate equal to one Hiroshima every three weeks. The development of techniques to resolve the "small" wars of the world must become one of mankind's foremost priorities.

This book has the following aims:

> To describe what I call the "crisis of illegitimate sovereignty" that is gripping the planet and to identify its principal components.
>
> To identify the circumstances and conditions wherein a plebiscite or an internationally supervised election could assist in resolving sovereignty crises.
>
> To discuss in detail the practical mechanics of conducting a plebiscite--based upon the lessons learned from two centuries of experimentation with the technique.
>
> This book is not a history of the plebiscite. Those wishing to examine case-by-case histories can refer to the excellent work of Mattern and Wambaugh. United Nations Trusteeship Council documents and the reports of the several Commonwealth Observer Groups are also of value to historical researchers.

A wide spectrum of people have lent their help and encouragement in the preparation of this book. My thanks go to Dr. T.H.R. Cashmore of the Foreign and Commonwealth Office in London who was a member of the Commonwealth Observer Group at the Uganda elections of 1980. My profound gratitude goes to the late Dr. Josef Korbel, a member of the United Nations Commission on India and Pakistan (UNCIP), which sought to arrange a plebiscite in Kashmir in the late 1940s and early 1950s. Special thanks go to Dr. Mark Imber of the University of St. Andrews and the International Politics Association of the University of St. Andrews for providing a forum for the airing of some of the ideas developed in this volume. Thanks are in order to Professor Grzegorz Seidler and the staff of Marie Curie Sklodowska University in Lublin, Poland, for their kindness and support during my half-year residence in Lublin in 1981.

The author is indebted to librarians and museum

personnel in several post-World War One plebiscite sites: Tonder, Denmark (Schleswig); Olsztyn, Poland (Allenstein and Marienwerder); Klagenfurt, Austria (the Klagenfurt Basin); and Saarbrucken, West Germany (the Saar).

I owe my initial interest in plebiscites to my grandmother, Cecelia Jochimsen, a native of Schleswig, who was born in Humptrup and was raised a few kilometers away in Saed. The 1920 plebiscite in Schleswig placed Humptrup in Germany and Saed in Denmark--an arrangement happily accepted by the residents to this day.

This author and all serious students of the plebiscite are deeply indebted to the pioneering work of Sarah Wambaugh whose thoughtful research into the post-World War One plebiscites represents political science at its best.

Thanks go to my colleagues in the Department of History, Political Science, and Economics at Lock Haven University for the congenial environment they have provided--especially John Washburn, James Knauer, Nelson Delavan, Edward Chatterton, and Francis Perna. Special thanks go to Professor John W. Johnston--the prince of department chairmen.

The encouragement and support of my wife, Deborah, has been essential throughout this project.

Finally, I am grateful for my year as Visiting Scholar at the Glasgow College of Technology. Especially helpful were Roger Carey (Head) and Roger Charlton of the Politics Department, David Donald and Alan Hutton of the Policy Analysis Research Unit, and Ron Burns of the Computer Services Unit. The College provided the time and the congenial atmosphere that made the writing of this book possible.

Lawrence T. Farley
Glasgow, Scotland

Plebiscites and Sovereignty

1

Introduction: The Crisis of Illegitimate Sovereignty

One of the chief sources of turmoil in the closing years of the twentieth century is a phenomenon which may be called "The Crisis of Illegitimate Sovereignty." The manifestations of this crisis--civil wars, secessionist struggles, wars of national liberation, irredentist movements--clutter the back pages of the daily press with reports of violence and unrest. While the posturings of the major powers fill the headlines it is the crisis of illegitimate sovereignty that fills the graveyards of the world. It is this crisis--seen in East Timor, Afghanistan, Israel (Palestine), Somalia, Namibia, Poland, Sri Lanka, Eritrea, Kampuchea, and in dozens of other troublespots--that both feeds and is fed by the Cold War between the superpowers. At the heart of the crisis are two concepts that define the essential political reality of our era: political legitimacy and national self-determination.

POLITICAL LEGITIMACY

The concept of political legitimacy addresses the question: Why do citizens obey their governments? It explains why citizens are willing to accept voluntarily the rules promulgated by their governments. Without legitimacy, a government must resort to methods of coercion: police, prisons, networks of informers, armies. Compulsion is not only costly and dangerous to governments that employ it but it breeds a livelier perception of political illegitimacy--particularly when minority economic or ethnic groups feel the sting of repression.

The perceived right of a government to rule can stem

from several sources: the sanction of God, aristocratic right, or the will of the people.

Divine Right

The "divine right of kings" principle has been a powerful source of legitimation throughout the world up into the twentieth century. Indeed, the expression "dei gratia"--"by the grace of God"--continues to appear on the coinage of the United Kingdom. The "mandate of heaven" has been an important element in the legitimacy of Chinese leaders for several millenia as has the divinity of the Japanese Emperor. Vestiges of the divine right principle remain. Many Islamic republics have achieved a synthesis of the divine right principle with other principles of legitimacy. Even in secular states such as the United States there are traces of divine legitimation. For instance, nearly every major presidential address is brought to a close by a ritual reference to the deity.

Aristocratic Right

Wisdom and virtue are significant sources of legitimacy. From Plato to Lenin, the possession of superior wisdom has been a major source of legitimacy. The idea is simple. If the "best" people are the rulers it is only sensible that they should be obeyed. If the most honest, capable, skilled, and far-sighted of our fellow citizens are piloting the "ship of state," should we not follow their rules and decisions? The answer, of course, is that regimes composed of small bodies of "wise men" tend to become self-serving oligarchies. Nevertheless, the continuing importance of the aristocratic principle can be seen in the "Revolutionary Command Councils" that follow upon military coups and in the elite role of communist parties in most Marxist-Leninist countries. The United States Senate, a small body removed from the popular will by a six year term in office, was meant by the founders of the Republic to be a chamber of wisemen with whom the president could consult on matters of state.

The Will of the People

The most important contemporary source of political legitimacy--the one that sharply distinguishes the twentieth century from all previous centuries--is the will of the people. Nearly every regime in the world today--be it a one-man dictatorship, a one-party totalitarian state, or a liberal multi-party democracy--claims to represent the will of its people. Rule of, by, and for the people has become the common denominator of politics in the world today. While this popular ideal is widely unrealized in practice, it is nevertheless a primary motivational force for change in every political system.

The "will of the people" as the bedrock of political legitimacy is the product of a thousand year trend toward greater participation in government. Centuries ago less than one percent of the inhabitants of countries around the world could be said to have participated in governmental decision-making. The concept of citizenship applied only to a very few. Gradually, merchants, craftsmen, independent farmers, and other categories of inhabitants achieved limited rights of participation in the governance of European states. Ultimately, the working class, landless peasants, ex-slaves, and women attained the prerogatives of voting and of holding public office. Today, across the world, adult inhabitants claim as a matter of right what were once the guarded privileges of the few. Every regime, from the most tyrannical dictatorship to the most saintly democracy, claims the "will of the people" as its license to rule.

What has changed in the waning years of the twentieth century is not the attachment of the world's people to the concept of rule by the people but an increasing sophistication regarding the means, procedures, and techniques of popular rule. Rule simply "in the name of the people" or rule simply "for" the people has come under increased attack. There are growing demands that practice should match rhetoric. Notions such as "participatory democracy" and "accountability" are rapidly changing global attitudes toward popular government. These new criteria for democracy are being applied to many of the planet's governments and many are found wanting. In country after country, in the North and the South, in the East and the West, the legitimacy of governments is being questioned.

NATIONAL SELF-DETERMINATION

National self-determination is the principle that a people has the right to decide the question of what state shall govern it. The principle arose out of the doctrine of "no conquests" proclaimed by the French revolutionaries of the 1790s.[1] It was viewed as an elementary "right of man" that allegiance may not be forced upon a people solely on the basis of decisions reached on the battlefield. Hence, the "right of conquest" was to be replaced by the right of peoples to determine freely their political affiliations. The French revolutionaries put the principle into practice by conducting plebiscites in territories captured by French armies. While seriously flawed by today's standards, these plebiscites dramatized to the European world the doctrine that no annexations, no changes in sovereignty should be undertaken without the consent of the people involved.

In the nineteenth century the notion of national self-determination, together with the concept of democracy, caught the imagination of subject nations throughout Europe. E.H. Carr has written:

> In this triumphal progress national self-determination and democracy went hand in hand. Self-determination might indeed be regarded as implicit in the idea of democracy; for if every man's right is recognised to be consulted about the affairs of the political unit to which he belongs, he may be assumed to have an equal right to be consulted about the form and extent of the unit.[2]

Nonetheless, the nineteenth century was an era of colonialism and of empire building. The governments of the major European powers ruled by divine and aristocratic right with only grudging acceptance of a role for the popular will.

The exigencies of the First World War brought national self-determination to the center of the world stage. First, the Central Powers (Germany, Austria-Hungary, and Ottoman Turkey) were multi-national empires filled with politically conscious subject nations (e.g., Poles, Czechs, Slovaks, Croatians, Arabs) chafing under "alien" rule. The Western allies readily saw that promises of national self-determination to these nations would encourage them to fight their imperial masters and thereby aid the Western cause.

Secondly, under the prodding of President Woodrow Wilson, the Allies proclaimed the principle of national self-determination as an official war aim. While not, as is commonly thought, part of the Fourteen Points, the principle was developed by Wilson in several major speeches:

> No peace can last, or ought to last, which does not recognize and accept the principle that governments derive all their just powers from the consent of the governed and that no right anywhere exists, to hand peoples about from sovereignty to sovereignty as if they were property.
>
> Peoples and provinces are not to be bartered about from sovereignty to sovereignty as if they were mere chattels and pawns in the game . . . Peoples may now be dominated and governed only by their own consent. Self-determination is not a mere phrase. It is an imperative principle of action, which statesmen will henceforth ignore at their peril.
>
> The settlement of every question, whether of territory, of sovereignty, of economic arrangement, or of political relationship, (must be) upon the basis of the free acceptance of that settlement by the people immediately concerned, and not upon the basis of the material interest or advantage of any other nation or people which may desire a different settlement for the sake of its own exterior influence or mastery.[3]

European statesmen, with varying degrees of enthusiasm, endorsed the principle as the premier objective of the war. Some of the most vigorous support for the principle came from a not wholly welcome quarter. The first proclamation of the Bolshevik regime, the Decree of Peace, approved by the Second All-Russia Congress of Soviets of Workers', Soldiers' and Peasants' Deputies on 26 October/8 November 1917, promised "guarantees to all nations dwelling in Russia and the genuine right to self-determination."[4] (Practice aside, the Soviet Union has remained loyal to the principle in terms of constitutional theory. The member republics of the U.S.S.R. retain the constitutional right to secede from the U.S.S.R.)

Following the First World War, the victorious allies (the Allied and Associated Powers) and their successor, the League of Nations, grappled at great length with what was called the "Minorities Problem." Petitions and delegations from dozens of distressed nationalities flooded the meeting halls and anterooms of Paris and Geneva. Investigative commissions composed of demographers and economists were dispatched to over a dozen localities. In some cases new states were created (e.g., Czechoslovakia, Yugoslavia). In others, borders were rectified to follow demographic lines or that reflected the will of the inhabitants as expressed in plebiscites (e.g., Schleswig, Allenstein and Marienwerder, Spisz and Orawa, Klagenfurt Basin, Sopron, Upper Silesia).

Outside of Europe a system of mandates was established in the colonies stripped from the Germans and Ottoman Turks. While a step forward in terms of respecting the rights of colonial peoples, the principle of national self-determination remained applicable only to White Europeans. Nevertheless, the First World War and its aftermath marked a turning point in the practical acceptance of the principle by the states of Europe. Speaking in 1929, the German Foreign Minister, Dr. Stresemann, signaled this acceptance:

> The greater the respect and protection accorded to men and women in the exercise of their inalienable right to preserve and use their mother-tongue, develop their civilisation and practice their religion irrespective of political frontiers, the less likely is it that international peace will be disturbed. No one can, by defending this idea, lay himself open to the charge of bringing about the disintegration of a State . . .[5]

World War Two marked the broadening of the principle to encompass all peoples around the globe. The right of national self-determination became the watch-word of the post-war period. Within two decades it had become enshrined in countless resolutions of the United Nations and in solemn declarations of nearly all states. Gradually, the principle has seeped into the consciousness of peoples in all corners of the planet.

SOVEREIGNTY AND THE STATE SYSTEM

While the "will of the people" as the fundamental

source of political legitimacy and the right of national self-determination have become virtual self-evident truths during the past century, they have had little impact on the rules of the state system--on the way states actually play the game of international politics.

States are the recognized actors in international politics--not nations. Indeed, it is inaccurate and misleading to use expressions such as "international politics," "international law," and "international organization." We live in a world of interstate politics, interstate law, and interstate organization. Nations (typically ethnic groups each with a common language and a common sense of community) differ from states in one vitally important way: states possess the attribute of sovereignty.[6] Nationhood is a demographic and psychological phenomenon; statehood is a formal-legal phenomenon. Only states, that is, possessors of sovereignty, may become members of the state system.

Sovereignty

Centuries ago in Europe monarchs were part of a hierarchical system of allegiance based upon the feudal model of vassalage. Bound by mutual rights and obligations, the king was subordinate to the emperor, the duke to the king, and so forth. This system broke-down under the impact of the Reformation when Roman Catholic emperors fought their Protestant kings and Roman Catholic kings fought their Protestant dukes. So bitter were Europe's religious wars that upwards of a third of the population of some areas perished. Ultimately, a compromise solution was achieved at the Peace of Westphalia in 1648. This compromise established the modern state system that remains to this day.

The key to the state system devised at Westphalia is the concept of sovereignty. In order to possess sovereignty, a regime must possess (1) territory, (2) population, and (3) it must be able to maintain a modicum of order within its territory and among its people. Finally, (4) the regime must be recognized as sovereign by states already possessing sovereignty. Under the Westphalian formula, sovereign states have three absolute prerogatives: independence, equality, and unanimity. Independence means a state is completely free to organize any system of government, proclaim an official religion of its choice, and structure its economy as it sees fit. No outside state, as in pre-Westphalian times, has any right to interfere in these strictly internal matters. Equality means every state is of equal rank with every other state. Empires do not outrank kingdoms. Kingdoms do not outrank duchies. All are equal. No state is legally subordinate to any other state. Unanimity means that no state is bound by the majority decisions reached by groups of states. A state is bound only if it agrees to be bound (hence, "unanimity"). Even then, a state, exercising the principle of rebus sic stantibus (changed circumstances), may later renege on an agreement.

The practical effect of the Westphalian formula is to compartmentalize the planet into separate and distinct sovereign states each of which have exclusive and unfettered authority within their borders. Sovereignty is, therefore, the defining characteristic of the modern state system. The concept of sovereignty sets out the ground rules of interstate relations. Those territorial entities that possess sovereignty belong to the world's most privileged and exclusive club--the club of states. As James has pointed out, there are many entities that do not possess sovereignty, for instance, Hong Kong, Bavaria, Greenland, and Connecticut.[7] There are many nations that dearly wish to have sovereign states of their own, e.g., the Palestinians, the Kurds, the Eritreans. James asserts:

> Sovereignty is therefore the ground rule of interstate relations in that it identifies the territorial entities who are eligible to participate in the game.
>
> There is, perhaps, no reason in principle why participation in international relations should not be open to any group (or, indeed, individual) which can, as it were, elbow its way on to the stage. But in practice social life in all contexts tends to give rise to the ordering mechanisms of categorization. Some are eligible to do this and go there, others not; nationals take this gate, aliens that; sheep on the right hand, goats on the left.[8]

Those nations that have acquired control of states--those who have acquired membership in the club of states--possess remarkable powers. Club members respect the right of other members to establish armies, police forces, courts, and prisons. In keeping with the Westphalian formula, members may forcibly impose religious or political ideologies upon their citizens and control the distribution of wealth. The club of states is, in essence, a "gun club" in which members and only members have the right to produce or purchase firearms from each other and to discharge these firearms within their respective borders at their sole discretion. States are the only organizations that are, in effect, licensed by the world community to kill.

Clearly, nations which do not possess states of their own and which find themselves within the boundaries of states controlled by other nationalities are at a severe disadvantage. Nations which control states have the Westphalian right to total domestic freedom of action including the use of force to protect and to further their interests. Stateless nations live at the mercy of nations that control states.

Several decades ago only a few dozen nations controlled states of their own. Today, over thirteen dozen have joined the club of states. Sovereignty is a dry, legal question for those nations who have acquired statehood. Sovereignty is a passionate cause for those who do not have it. The recent proliferation of microstates has stimulated further the desire of small nations to gain entrance to the club. "If Tuvalu can join, why can't we?" At the present time there are over fifty separatist, irredentist, and national liberation movements in the world demanding either new states or a redrawing of the boundaries of existing states. States that are politically and militarily dominated by their neighbors, e.g., Poland (U.S.S.R.), Kampuchea (Vietnam), Lesotho (South Africa), are accorded sovereign status by most club members only as a matter of courtesy. These peoples as well as those who see themselves as victims of foreign economic imperialism clamor for a return to genuine sovereignty in the full Westphalian sense of the term.

ILLEGITIMATE SOVEREIGNTY

As the last fragments of overseas empire are dissolved and as the United Nations Trusteeship Council concludes its business, the statesmen of the world are writing "FINISHED" on the checkerboard of existing states. The traditional prerogatives of sovereignty are being asserted with unparalleled vigor. With few exceptions the nationalist movements that rode to statehood on the principle of national self-determination have now all but renounced the principle in favor of the Westphalian dogma of "territorial integrity." As will be discussed later, a status quo or "holy alliance" psychology has emerged in the past decade in which existing states--less two--are imagined to be the final product of the historical process. The two exceptions (Israel and South Africa) in which national self-determination (for the Palestinians and for the Blacks of southern Africa) is being placed above sovereign prerogative are viewed as vestiges of the colonial past--as unfinished business. Once concluded, the era of achievement of national self-determination will be at an end.

Such is the trend of thinking among statesmen. It runs in direct contradiction to the most important political trends of our time. It ignores the growing number of illegitimate governments--regimes that are viewed by substantial portions of their population as illegal, foreign dictatorships. Ethnic minorities, chafing under blatantly discriminatory "nation-building" and "assimilationist" policies are abandoning peaceful, internal solutions in exchange for violent separatist and "national liberation" struggles. Never before have demands for genuine representative government "by the people" and for self-determination by stateless ethnic groups been so widespread. Never before have distressed minorities had such ready access to quantities of advanced weaponry.

Thus, the global community is embroiled in a crisis of illegitimate sovereignty. There is a lack of congruence between the official, legal elements of the system--states--and the operative political elements of the system--nations. There is a major imbalance of power between the two elements with one--the states--enforcing an exclusive right to armies, police, and prisons.

MANIFESTATIONS OF THE CRISIS OF ILLEGITIMATE SOVEREIGNTY

Secessionist and Irredentist Movements

Secessionist and irredentist movements are a principal manifestation of illegitimate sovereignty. A secessionist movement is one that seeks to separate a population from an existing state in order to form a new state. The residents of Quebec who seek separation from the Canadian federation and independence for Quebec are members of a separatist movement. An irredentist movement occurs when a population in one state seeks to break away from that state in order to unite with their fellow nationals in a neighboring state. German-speaking "Tyrolians" in northern Italy who seek reunification with their fellow Germans in Austria are an example of an irredentist movement.

Secessionist and irredentist movements become possible when ethnic groups begin to perceive themselves as nations. Smith has developed the concept of ethnic nationalism as the essential bridge between ethnicity and statehood:

> Ethnic nationalism has striven to turn the ethnic group into that more abstract and politicised category, the 'nation,' and then to establish the latter as the sole criterion of statehood. Its lack of success to date in securing such 'national congruence' has not deterred nationalists from pursuing their ideals or from spawning new separatist movements in every continent. Though it has many powerful opponents, the ideal of the nation has been generalised to encompass a vast number of ethnic communities, large and small, and now exerts considerable pressure upon the global system of states which has been constructed with scant reference to the aspirations of ethnic communities and ethnic nationalism.[9]

The second half of the twentieth century has seen an expansion in the number of states but an explosion in the number of ethnic groups that have discovered (or rediscovered) their sense of nationality and have begun to crave membership in the club of states.

A partial list of current separatists and irredentist movements reveals the extent of this explosion:

ASIA	EUROPE
Ainu (Japan)	Albanians (Yugoslavia)
Armenians (Turkey)	Basques (Spain)
Azerbaijanis (Iran-U.S.S.R.)	Bretons (France)
Baluchis (Pakistan)	Catalans (Spain)
Chaldeans (Iraq)	Corsicans (France)
East Timorese (Indonesia)	Croatians (Yugoslavia)
Hmongs (Laos)	Estonians (U.S.S.R.)

Kachins (Burma)
Karens (Burma)
Kashmiris (India-Pakistan)
Kurds (Turkey-Iran-Iraq)
Mizos (India)
Moros (Philippines)
Nagas (India)
Palestinians (Israel-Jordan)
Pathans (Pakistan)
Sikhs (India)
Shans (Burma)
Sindhis (Pakistan)
South Moluccans (Indonesia)
Taiwanese (China)
Tamils (India-Sri Lanka)
Tibetans (China)
Turkmens (Iran-U.S.S.R.)

AFRICA

Eritreans (Ethiopia)
Ewe (Ghana-Togo)
Ovambos (Angola)
Saharauis (Morocco)
Shabans-Katangese (Zaire)
Somalis (Ethiopia)
Tigreans (Ethiopia)

Greeks (Cyprus)
Hungarians (Rumania)
Irish (U.K.)
Karelians (Finland-U.S.S.R.)
Lapps (Sweden)
Latvians (U.S.S.R.)
Lithuanians (U.S.S.R.)
Scots (U.K.)
Slovaks (Czechoslovakia)
Slovenes (Austria)
Turks (Cyprus)
Tyrolians (Italy)
Ukrainians (U.S.S.R.)
Welsh (U.K.)
Wends (East Germany)

THE AMERICAS

Amerindians (U.S.A.)
Greenlanders (Denmark)
Puerto Ricans (U.S.A.)
Quebecois (Canada)

Historically, Europe, the most politicized of the continents in terms of national identifications, has led the world in the number of secessionist and irredentist movements. However, in terms of growth, Asia and Africa pose the greatest challenge. For example, each of the 54 states in Africa (including Namibia) has an average of 8 million people, 55 ethnic groups, and over a dozen languages.[10]

Just as the fission and fusion of atoms unleashes immense energy, so too does secessionism and irredentism release vast quantities of political distress upon the members of the state system. Cobban has asserted that "nationalism has passed from the stage of state-making to that of state-breaking. The newer nation-states of Asia and Africa have hardly even had the time to be born before reproducing the situation, which it used to be thought was peculiar to imperial regimes, of two or more nations warring in the bosom of a single state."[11] Of the approximately 28 wars being fought around the world in the mid-1980s, half are the direct product of secessionist and irredentist struggles. (Most of the rest are also the result of perceptions of illegitimate sovereignty caused by foreign occupation, e.g., Afghanistan, Kampuchea.)

The hopes of many disaffected, stateless nationalities have been raised by the current proliferation of micro-states. Micro-states, defined as having less than two million inhabitants, are coming into existence at a rate of several per year as the last fragments of the European colonial empires are made into independent states. By the year 2000 A.D. micro-states are expected to comprise one fourth of the membership of the United Nations.[12] Seeing that dozens of other small nationalities have joined the club of sovereign states, the demand for sovereignty is increasing among the disaffected nations within the world's many multi-national states.

Another phenomenon that is fueling the demand for sovereignty has been the successful participation of small states in regional economic organizations and in regional military alliances. If Singapore can be a leader of the ASEAN group, if Luxembourg can enjoy the benefits of membership in the European Community and in NATO, why should not other small states be capable of succeeding as well?

TERRORISM

Another manifestation of the crisis of illegitimate sovereignty is the growing level of terrorism conducted by secessionist, irredentist, and national liberation movements. Not a day passes without reports of kidnappings, assassinations, hijackings, bombings, or sabotage. Indeed, so commonplace is terrorism that it has become part of the "background noise" of contemporary world affairs.

Instances of criminal terrorism (terror for profit) and of ideological terrorism (terror for ideas) are dwarfed in number by instances of ethnic group terrorism. Existing secessionist, irredentist, and national liberation movements have spawned over a hundred liberation armies and terror squads. While many of these units sound faintly ridiculous to cosmopolitan Western ears, they pursue their enemies in deadly earnest. For instance, the obscure "Armenian Secret Army for the Liberation of Armenia" and its allies have been credited with the killing of thirty and the wounding of eighty-nine

Turkish diplomats and officials between 1973 and 1982.[13]

The term "terrorism" is a label applied by states to the violent activities of non-state groups. Non-state groups call such activity "legitimate self-defense," "freedom fighting," and "liberation struggle." The problem, however, is much deeper than that of terminology. In the state system of the post-Westphalian era, each state is entitled to possess and employ instruments of coercion within its territory. Hence, in the pursuit of the public interest and in the maintenance of public order, states recognize the sovereign right of other states to use force. States, therefore, do not "kidnap" their citizens, they "arrest" then. They do not "assassinate," they judiciously "execute." They do not "hijack," they "impound." Under the spell of this dual nomenclature, a national leader can be a "terrorist" to some observers and a "freedom fighter" to others. A pre-independence "traitor" can become a post-independence "statesman." The key to this remarkable polarity is, of course, membership or non-membership in the club of states. It is little wonder that oppressed and brutalized nationalities the world over are beating down the door to this the most privileged club of all.

GENOCIDE

One all too obvious response by states to the crisis of illegitimate sovereignty is the "final solution" of genocide. Genocide, the murder of some or all of a national or ethnic group, is an attractive method of state control primarily because of its conceptual simplicity. The recorded history of the human race is filled with instances of systematic genocide or genocide through policies of ruthless neglect. The horror evoked by the tragedy of the Armenians and of the Jews in the first half of the twentieth century has led many to believe that genocide has become extinct and unthinkable as an instrument of policy. The evidence is quite to the contrary.

While claims of genocide are always subject to dispute (many Turks and some Germans to this day claim there was no policy of genocide directed against the Armenians and the Jews), there have been several credible instances of genocide recently:

In Indonesia against the Chinese minority in the late 1960s.
In Nigeria against the Ibos in 1966-1968.
In Pakistan against the Bengalis in 1971.
In Burundi against the Hutus in 1972-1973.
In Iran against the Kurds in 1975-1977.[14]

Yet blood need not be spilt for genocide to play an important role in the control and suppression of dissident minority groups. Credible threats of genocide (e.g., President Amin's threat to the Asian population of Uganda in the early 1970s) and an intense fear of genocide (e.g., the Miskito Indians of Nicaragua in the early 1980s) are readily exploited by states as a means of intimidating minority populations. Indeed, threats of genocide are one of the factors underlying the explosion in the number of refugees during the past decade.

There is no evidence that policies of genocide carried-out by states in the twentieth century have succeeded in resolving the problem of dissident minorities. On the contrary, such policies appear to have created generations of fanatics utterly devoted to their respective national causes and ferociously intolerant of the legitimate aspirations of other nationalities.

Policies of genocide--or simply of mass indiscriminate killing of civilians--generate waves of refugees. All wars create refugees. But separatist wars and wars of national liberation--historically among the bloodiest of wars--tend to breed great numbers of long-term refugees. The reason is clear. Governments, members of the gun club of states, typically possess a vast superiority in firepower over their dissident opponents. Even a modest use of modern heavy weapons against disaffected populations will generate terror, panic, and flight. According to the United Nations High Commissioner for Refugees, the world is in the throws of a refugee epidemic.[15] People are fleeing from their illegitimate governments in record numbers. Thus, the flood of refugees is yet another manifestation of the crisis of illegitimate sovereignty.

HOLY ALLIANCES

The term "holy alliance" has come to mean a status quo alliance in which the members promise to render reciprocal assistance or collective action to suppress change. The original "Holy Alliance," a vaguely worded document instigated by Tsar Alexander I in 1815, pledged unspecified forms of "reciprocal service" to be rendered by the crowned heads of the "Christian nation."[16] The Holy Alliance came to be "regarded by European liberals as a hateful compact of despots against the liberties of mankind" since it was used to justify the suppression of republican revolutions.[17] For example, Austrian armies accomplished the spirit of the Holy Alliance in 1821 by overturning the revolutionary regimes in Piedmont and Naples and by restoring crowned heads to their respective thrones.

Diplomatic history is replete with status quo alliances of various sorts. The Monroe Doctrine may be viewed as a tacit pact between the United States and Great Britain to exclude the remaining European powers from the New World. The so-called Brezhnev Doctrine asserts that the fraternity of socialist states may act if members are threatened by anti-socialist counterrevolution. The Warsaw Pact intervention in Hungary (1956) and in Czechoslovakia (1968) were clear illustrations of a status quo alliance in practice.

The most pervasive if usually unspoken "holy alliance" of our time is that between members of the state system. The code word for this tacit status quo alliance is "territorial integrity," that is, new states may not be created out of the territory of existing states--with the exception of peoples under "colonial domination." The Organization of African Unity (OAU) has been unusually candid in this regard by asserting the inviolability of the existing African borders and denying any right of secession from existing African states.

President Tsirinana of the Malagasy Republic declared at an OAU summit in 1963:

> It is no longer possible, nor desirable, to modify the Boundaries of Nations, on the pretext of racial, religious or linguistic criteria. . . Indeed, should we take race, religion or language criteria for setting our boundaries, a few States in Africa would be blotted out from the map. Leaving demagogy aside, it is not conceivable that one of our individual States would readily consent to be among the victims, for the sake of Unity.

President Keita of Mali asserted that:

> we must take Africa as it is, and we must renounce all territorial claims, if we do not wish to introduce what we might call black imperialism in Africa . . . African unity demands of each one of us complete respect for the legacy we have received from the colonial system, that is to say: maintenance of the present frontiers of our respective states . . . respect for the territorial sovereignty and integrity of each state should be made concrete by an undertaking, a multilateral non-aggression pact guaranteed by each of the states gathered here.

A memorandum developed at the 1963 summit by the Kenyan delegation came directly to the point:

> The principle of self-determination has relevance where FOREIGN DOMINATION is the issue. It has no relevance where the issue is territorial disintegration by dissident citizens.[18]

The resolute behavior of most African states in assisting Zaire to suppress the Shaba (Katanga) separatists--even to the extent of welcoming the intervention of European troops--illustrates the overriding salience of the territorial integrity principle. However, there are a growing number of challenges to the inviolability of Africa's colonial borders and to the integrity of existing states as the more and more distressed ethnic groups become politicized and as the supply of weapons continues to expand.

Thus, the existing members of the club of states view the creation of new states in zero sum terms. Any new states must be created wholely at the expense of the current members--who stand to lose both territory and population. So great is the concern of states over the specter of separatism that "territorial integrity" has all but replaced "national self-determination" as the watch-word of the post-colonial era. One can even find United Nations General Assembly resolutions praising the Administering Powers of Trusteeship Territories for "discouraging separatist movements" among their charges and condemning Administering Powers that permit separatist movements.[19]

The fundamental flaw in all holy alliances to suppress secessionist and irredentist movements is the simple fact that states chronically meddle in each other's domestic politics. Statesmen are often compelled by internal pressures to pay heed to the problems of fellow nationals inhabiting other states. States wishing to undermine or destabilize the governments of unfriendly states often provide financial and weapons aid to separatist movements. Indeed, few separatist movements rise to prominence without the backing of helpful states. Thus, there is little prospect that holy alliances of states will succeed in containing the growing crisis of illegitimate sovereignty. Inter-state hostilities and rivalries are likely to undermine such alliances and to exacerbate the crisis.

COLONIALISM

The evolution of the term "colonialism" tells us much about the contemporary state system.

In the nineteenth century there were two types of colonialism: overseas and adjacent. Overseas colonialism was exemplified by the far-flung empires of Portugal, Spain, France, the Netherlands, and the United Kingdom. Adjacent colonialism was seen in the empires of Austria, Russia, and Ottoman Turkey. In the early twentieth century the great adjacent colonial empires were either dissolved (the Austrian and the Ottoman Empires) or reorganized into a "progressive" federation (the Russian Empire). Thus, adjacent colonialism had all but vanished decades before the great era of decolonization: 1945-1975. Hence, "colonialism" in the eyes of both the developed and underdeveloped world today means "overseas colonialism," i.e., colonialism occurs when a nation is dominated by a state which is LOCATED OVERSEAS. The domination of a nation by another--especially if the two are located within the boundaries of one state--is not labelled "colonialism." To suggest that such domination is a form of colonialism opens one to charges of undermining the state's territorial integrity.

It is instructive to note that Israel and South Africa, while dominating adjacent nations, still qualify as colonialists because they are viewed by the majority of United Nations member states as manifestations of European--hence overseas--colonialism. The Falkland-Malvinas Islands are widely regarded as colonial possessions of the United Kingdom but would not be so regarded under Argentine rule because they are adjacent to Argentina and overseas from Britain. The issue is one of sovereign territorial integrity for Argentina--not of self-determination for the islanders.

Thus, the currently accepted definition of colonialism utterly fails to reflect the realities of the existing state system--a system in which only 10 percent of the states are ethnically homogeneous and where nearly 40 percent are multi-national states where NO nationality comprises a majority of the population. Adjacent colonialism--called by some scholars "internal colonialism"--is the order of the day in much of the world.[20]

COSMOPOLITAN INTERNATIONALISM

There is a strong tendency among the "mature" nations of the West--nations that have settled comfortably into statehood--to view with disdain the clamorous and often violent nationalisms of other peoples. "Grow up!" is the advice offered by weary Westerners. "The future lies with international cooperation, mutual interdependence, and a recognition of our common humanity. Don't be such fools as to repeat our centuries of nationalist squabbling and gratuitous bloodshed."

This approach, which may be called "cosmopolitan internationalism," identifies nationalism as the root cause of the world's suffering. The solution to the problem of nationalism is to dissolve nationalism by persuading nations--especially those who are stateless--to embrace internationalism. The wars of the twentieth century, wars that have killed over 100 million people, are seen as the product of nationalism. It is thought that the maldistribution of wealth in the world is reinforced and exacerbated by nationalism. Attempts at essential international cooperation are undermined by nationalism. When international organizations such as the European Community founder on some devisive issue, the culprit is invariably nationalism, e.g., "Those damned French!" Thus, the entire catalogue of the world's miseries is laid at the doorstep of "nationalism."

The evidence speaks quite to the contrary. The heart of the world's woe is political illegitimacy. The stable, prosperous corners of the planet are those where national aspirations are fulfilled by appropriate state structures.

Illegitimate regimes imposing their authority upon unwilling communities are the midwives of nationalist revolution.

CONCLUSION: AN ERA OF POLITICAL ILLEGITIMACY

We are living in a era of political illegitimacy--perhaps the most politically illegitimate era in human history. The reasons are plainly evident:

The millenial trend toward greater citizen participation in public affairs continues to broaden and deepen.

Deriving from this trend, the "Will of the People" has become the paramount source of political legitimacy throughout the world.

The world's people continue to subdivide themselves into nations and to demand that their will be expressed via nationally defined states.

The post-Westphalian state system is fundamentally resistant to these trends and lends sanction to the violent suppression of those contesting the illegitimate sovereignty of many existing states.

How can this crisis of legitimacy be resolved? One course is to allow the darwinian process to continue with the strong or lucky nations surviving and the weak or unlucky being destroyed or assimilated. This course may well require centuries of struggle and, given the proliferation of fissionable and other substances of apocalyptic destruction, may entail the devastation of much of our planet.

The other course is to develop and apply techniques of political legitimation--techniques of conflict resolution that allow citizen participation the key role in the establishment of political structures. One such technique is the international plebiscite.

NOTES

1. Johannes Mattern, The Employment of the Plebiscite in the Determination of Sovereignty (Baltimore: The Johns Hopkins Press, 1920), p. 76.

2. Edward Hallett Carr, Conditions of Peace (New York: Macmillan, 1942), p. 39.

3. Mattern, p. 177.

4. U.O. Umozurike, Self-Determination in International Law (Hamden: Archon, 1972), p. 162.

5. Ten Years Life of the League of Nations (London: May Fair Press, 1929), p. 111.

6. The construction of an adequate definition of "nation" has eluded analysts for a century. "Nation" means one thing to an American (who tends to equate nation with state) and something quite different to an Ibo in Nigeria or a Lebanese in Costa Rica. Nevertheless, perceptions of nationality--of the community to which one belongs--are central to domestic and interstate politics. A taxpayer in Newcastle-upon-Tyne will view as proper and reasonable the payment of government welfare benefits to his fellow Englishman in London who is unemployed--even to a Welshman in Cardiff who is similarly out of work. Such payments to an unemployed worker in Belgium could cause problems for our Newcastle taxpayer. If he perceives the political community to which he belongs as being "European," then the Belgian is a fellow citizen in much the same sense as a Londoner. If he perceives himself to be "British," then the only legitimate assistance to the Belgian would have to take the form of "foreign aid." The Newcastle taxpayer would certainly bridle at any suggestion that his tax contributions should provide the same benefits to the Tanzanian or Burmese unemployed as to his fellow Britains or, perhaps, Europeans. Perceptions of nationality are even more pivotal in matters of defense and security. The line separating "them" from "us" on defense issues is always much closer to home than on economic issues. Thus, the sense of nationality is a fundamental behavioral fact of political life.

7. Alan James, "Sovereignty: Ground Rule or Gibberish?" A paper prepared for the Annual Conference of the British International Studies Association, Southampton, England, 16-17 December 1982, pp. 4-5.

8. James, p. 2 and p. 9.

9. Anthony D. Smith, The Ethnic Revival (Cambridge: Cambridge University Press, 1981), p. xii.

10. Willie J. Breytenbach, "The Salience of African Ethno-Cultural Pluralism with Regard to Democratic Conflict Resolution and Intergroup Accommodation." A paper prepared for the Conference on Southern African Affairs, Institute for Plural Societies, Pretoria University, New York, NY, 23-25 October 1978, p. 1.

11. Alfred Cobban, The Nation-State and National Self-Determination, Revised Edition (New York: Thomas Y. Crowell, 1969), p. 17.

12. The Stanley Foundation, "Decision-Making Processes of the United Nations," Ninth Conference on the United Nations of the Next Decade, Vail, Colorado, June 1974, pp. 13-14.

13. "Terror," International Herald Tribune, 16 November 1982, p. 7.

14. The Heritage Foundation (Washington), "SA is Victim of Double Standards," South African Digest (13 August 1982), p. 14.

An illustration of attempted cultural genocide is provided by Jonathan Mirsky: "After the 1959 flight of the Dalai Lama, Mao's proconsuls in Tibet, which occupies a sixth of the entire land area of the People's Republic, set about eradicating the native culture of the 'autonomous region.'

Purportedly to liberate Tibetans from their 'feudal past,' the Chinese forbade Buddhism and the written language. Tibetans were given Chinese names. Even barley, the traditional staple food, was replaced by wheat, in compliance with a Maoist obsession that throughout China, whatever the conditions, wheat must become 'the key link.'" "How Tibet Survived the Red Guards," The Observer (London), 3 July 1983, p. 5.

15. Iain Guest, "UN Refugee Body to Study Ways of Protecting Camps from Attack," International Herald Tribune, 27 April 1983, p. 2. There are presently about 10.3 million refugees receiving assistance from the UNHCR.

16. A.J. Grant and Harold Temperly, Europe in the Nineteenth and Twentieth Centuries (London: Longmans, Green and Company, 1940), p. 179.

17. Grant and Temperley, p. 179.

18. Rupert Emerson, From Empire to Nation: The Rise to Self-Assertion of Asian and African Peoples (Cambridge: Harvard University Press, 1962), p. 34. A decade after serving as midwife to the birth of Bangladesh (formerly eastern Pakistan), Prime Minister Indira Gandhi proclaimed "We are against any secessionist movement in any sovereign country. India . . . does not want to interfere in the internal affairs of any other country." Quoted in "Sri Lanka Imposes National Curfew After Rioting, Massacre of Prisoners," International Herald Tribune, 27 July 1983, p. 1.

19. "Papua New Guinea," U.N. Monthly Chronicle, Vol. XI, No. 1 (1974), p. 44.

U.S. Ambassador to the United Nations Donald F. McHenry addressed the problem in 1980: "I wish to reiterate also that although my Government regrets the decision of the Micronesians to seek separate political identities, and my personal opposition to separatism in the Trust Territory is long-standing and well-known, the United States shares the view of the Trusteeship Council that it is ultimately for the Micronesians themselves to decide upon their future political relations with one another. It must also be noted that, although unity is the desired objective, there have been other instances in which Trust Territories have emerged from Trusteeship disunited." Letter dated 8 May 1980 from the Permanent Representative of the United States of America to the United Nations addressed to the Secretary-General, T/1815, p. 1.

20. Smith, p. 30.

2

Background to the Plebiscite

The concept of plebiscite derives from the broader notion of popular sovereignty, or more simply, democracy. The place of the plebiscite in the democratic schema may be summarized thusly:

TYPES OF ELECTION	SPECIFIC FUNCTION
Candidate	
Primary	to choose party's candidates for General Election
General	to choose from among candidates for government posts
Runoff	to choose from among top vote-getters in previous election
Recall	to remove government officer from post
Issue	
Referendum	to approve or reject a proposal
Types of referenda include:	
Initiative	to approve or reject a proposal initiated by citizens directly (by-passing representative assemblies)

Plebiscite	to approve or reject a proposal concerning sovereignty

Plebiscite is a subset of the larger category referendum. A referendum is a type of issue election the function of which is to approve or reject a specified proposal. A plebiscite is a type of referendum wherein the proposal at issue concerns the matter of sovereignty. As a type of election, the plebiscite is one of many modes of political participation. Ultimately, it is the principle of popular right, of the "Will of the People" as the basis of political legitimacy, that accounts for the importance of all elections in the contemporary world. Governments receive their mandate to rule through the participatory involvement of the citizens. The plebiscite is but one form of citizen participation but it is the one wherein the citizen grapples with the institutional leviathan of our age--the sovereign state.

ORIGINS OF THE PLEBISCITE

The Ancient Heritage

It is generally recognized that the concept of democracy was first articulated in the Western world by the ancient Greeks. While the work of Greek philosophers is widely read, the practical contributions of the Greeks to the mechanics of democratic government are often ignored. Several of their contributions, especially in the area of parliamentary and balloting procedures, have echoed and reverberated through the centuries. For instance, the expression "to black ball" derives from the Greek practice of ostracism. An official (or any resident of a city) could be banished--ostracized--for a specified number of years if a majority of the citizenry voted him out. This was done by each citizen casting a stone--an <u>ostrakon</u> or "voting stone"--into an urn or basket. A white stone was cast if the voter was opposed to banishment, a black stone if in favor. Thus, the Greeks invented what is now called a "recall" election except that the offending official was not only stripped of office but expelled from the country as well.

The patricians of ancient Rome evolved structures that enabled those who paid taxes--themselves--to participate in government decision-making. During the early years of the Roman Republic the class of free commoners--the plebeians--also took a hand in decisions affecting their political and economic position. A plebiscitum was a resolution approved by an assembly of plebeians and, with certain important limitations, had the force of law. While the formal right of plebiscite was lost with the fall of the Roman Republic, the succeeding Roman emperors retained a healthy respect for the "city mob" that often participated in the violent making and breaking of emperors.

The fall of the Roman Empire and the political assertion of the Germanic and other "barbarian" tribes in Europe brought a vigorous reaffirmation of (what we would call) democratic values. From the perspective of Roman observers such as Tacitus, the Germanic tribes were democratic in the extreme.[1] Tumultuous tribal assemblies elected both political leaders and military commanders and, by clashing their shields together, voted on issues of war and peace. Seasoned with a strong dash of egalitarianism, the tribal assemblies elected individuals who could get the job done--be they servants, foreigners, or women--and then held them closely accountable. This tradition of participatory democracy was gradually supplanted throughout Europe by the divine right and aristocratic edifice of feudalism. Only in remote areas of Europe--in Scandinavia and in Switzerland--did the old traditions of popular democracy persist to become beacons of democracy in contemporary times.

Another early influence that helped to shape the Western concept of popular sovereignty was the essential egalitarianism of Christianity. While the official organization of the Christian Church adopted and has retained to this day the hierarchical structure--even the uniforms--of the Roman civil service, the basic message of the Church has always been one of human equality. All men and women, regardless of class or race, are equal in the eyes of God. All are born with original sin and all are capable of salvation. The profoundly political implications of such thorough-going egalitarianism have become clear only in the past century with the advent of Marxism.

A second important contribution of the Christian Church to the West's democratic heritage has been the Church's continuous encouragement of literacy. Christianity, like Judaism and Islam, bases its teachings upon a set of divinely inspired texts. Thus, to be a fully conversant Christian, one must be sufficiently literate to read and understand the books of the Bible and the teachings of the Church derived from the Bible. Consequently, the Church has been the principal underwriter of education in the West for the past two thousand years. Only in the past century have states, building upon the heritage of literacy cultivated by the Church, assumed the major role in providing education to the populace. Literacy and democracy are causally related. Increases in public participation in civic affairs are nearly always linked to greater levels of literacy. It is little wonder that in the early Middle Ages, when kings and lords were often unable to write their own names, that the wretched masses played no role whatever in government decision-making.

The Mediaeval Heritage

The feudal system, which debased the common people to the status of chattel and which gloried in hierarchy and class distinction, nevertheless contributed an essential element to the nascent democratic tradition. This element was the idea of a social contract. Human society was viewed as a network of contracts. Contracts may be negotiated. Contracts may be made and may be broken. The parties to a contract acquire both rights and obligations. Hence, both lord and vassal, ruler and ruled, are constrained by law. Charters--the forerunners to modern constitutions--were drawn-up in many parts of Europe to detail the mutual rights and obligations of kings and their vassals. Changes in the terms of a charter--or any contract--require the consent of the contracting parties. Thus, the Feudal Age contributed a key element to the evolving democratic tradition.

The Feudal Age was succeeded by the Age of Absolutism--a period in which kings sought to break the power of the gentry and to create a system of omnipotent central monarchies. The king, according to the theorists of absolute monarchy, was above the law. The king ruled by "the grace of God" and by virtue of the quintessential excellence of his aristocratic blood. It was at this time that the concepts of sovereignty and state were developed to reinforce the absolute supremacy of the monarch. (Thus, the modern state system was forged at a time of anti-democratic reaction.) However, the kings needed allies in the struggle against the entrenched nobility and found these allies in the expanding cities of Renaissance Europe. Merchants and craftsmen, desiring stable domestic markets and secure trade routes abroad, supported strong central monarchies. The kings, appreciative of the growing tax revenues provided by the cities, granted royal charters to the burghers--the citizens--of the large towns and cities. Once again, a set of contractual relationships developed wherein mutual rights and obligations governed the relationship between ruler and ruled. Gradually, the rising urban middle class, as the chief provider of state revenues, increased its "power of the purse" through representative bodies that in the course of time became the lower houses of modern European parliaments.

Not surprisingly, it was the burghers of the city of Geneva in 1420 who organized the first international plebiscite--a vote to determine sovereignty. The Duke of Savoy, having bought the County of Geneva (Comte de Genevois), decided to annex the city as well. His plan was unanimously rejected by an assembly of the inhabitants of Geneva--an assembly of churchmen, merchants, soldiers, craftsmen, lords, and laborers alike. It would appear to have been the first case of a plebiscite conducted by universal (male) suffrage. All the inhabitants "without exception and without distinction and all equal before the law" expressed themselves on a matter of sovereignty.[2] It was an unusual event for its time--all the more so because it proved successful in preventing the planned annexation. Henceforth, the cities of Europe--given their wealth, literacy, manpower, and often strong city fortifications--developed autonomous economic and political institutions of an increasingly democratic character. They were the first to express openly the principle of popular self-determination and, to a limited degree, carry it into practice.

The Eighteenth Century Heritage

The watershed in the evolution of the West's democratic heritage came in the eighteenth century. Our vocabulary of democratic principles and practices sprang from the revolutionary ferment of the period. The American Revolution of 1776 and the French Revolution of 1789 marked the coming of age of popular sovereignty. The principles enumerated by the representatives of the American colonies on July 4, 1776, could be the manifesto of dozens of separatist and national liberation movements today:

> When, in the course of human events, it becomes necessary for one people to dissolve the political bands which have connected them with another, and to assume, among the powers of the earth, the separate and equal station to which the laws of nature and of nature's God entitle them, a decent respect to the opinions of mankind requires that they should declare the causes which impel them to the separation.
>
> We hold these truths to be self-evident, that all men are created equal; that they are endowed by their Creator with certain unalienable rights; that among these are life, liberty, and the pursuit of happiness. That, to secure these rights, governments are instituted among men, deriving their just powers from the consent of the governed; that, whenever any form of government becomes destructive of these ends, it is the right of the people to alter or to abolish it, and to institute new government, laying its foundation on such principles, and organizing powers in such form, as to them shall seem most likely to effect their safety and happiness.[3]

The inhabitants of the American colonies were the first of many colonial peoples to proclaim the right of national self-determination.

It is one thing for colonists to endorse the concept of popular sovereignty. It is something quite else for the world's leading power--the Kingdom of France--to be overturned by zealous revolutionaries proclaiming the "rights of man." The rights published by the French revolutionaries were not simply the rights of Frenchmen. They were universal rights of all peoples. Thus, the French Constitutional Assembly enacted a decree in 1790 affirming that "the French nation renounces the undertaking of any war for the purpose of conquest, and that it will never employ its forces against the liberty of any people."

French armies soon found themselves in possession of new lands. If "conquest" is forbidden as an infringement of human rights, then what about annexation? The answer was the first systematic use of the international plebiscite. In town halls throughout those territories designated for annexation to France, registers were opened allowing all inhabitants the right to record their approval or disapproval. Another form of plebiscite consisted of the citizenry electing delegates--instructed delegates--to form a general assembly that would decide the issue of sovereignty. An excerpt from a French proclamation to the people of Savoy in 1792 reveals the flavor of such plebiscites.

> Brethren and friends: Rise from your lethargy; you owe to the French only esteem and recognition . . . while our armies guard your liberty, busy yourselves to make it secure. . .
>
> Proud of the success of our arms, we could give you orders, but the French Republic has effaced from its annals the words king, master and subjects . . . we only give you advice.
>
> Primary assemblies are the only kind in which the people can exercise their sovereignty.
>
> Hence, we exhort the free people of Savoy to gather to-day, peaceably, without weapons, under the guidance of the French arms, in each commune, in order to nominate a deputy charged to express in a general assembly their wish for a new government.[4]

Such plebiscites, often conducted under the partisan eyes of French occupation troops, fell far short of contemporary standards of fairness and secrecy. Nevertheless, they had a profound effect upon the political climate of their time. The citizen, after an absence of many centuries, was once again nominated for a role in the game of states.

Given the somewhat frenzied state of post-revolutionary French nationalism, the plebiscite was applied only to the joining of territory to France. It was considered treason--punishable by death--to so much as suggest the alienation of any portion of sovereign French soil. Thus the French Revolution, spread throughout the European continent by the campaigns of Napoleon, spread both the principle of popular sovereignty and the model of intense nationalism. Inspired by the French, nations from Finland to Greece commenced a century long period of democratic and nationalist agitation that produced over a dozen new states in Europe.

The Nineteenth Century Heritage

With the final collapse of Napoleon's Empire in 1814-1815 the international plebiscite fell into disuse for nearly half a century. (Indeed, Napoleon himself had ceased to apply the plebiscite to his more far-flung conquests.) Given the mortal fright administered to the royal aristocrats of Europe by the French revolutionaries and by Napoleon, a vigorous anti-democratic and anti-nationalist reaction set in. The Concert of Europe and, more grandiosely, the Holy Alliance, marked attempts by the crowned heads of Europe to stem the rising tide of democratic and nationalist activism. The lesser kingdoms and principalities of Europe--particularly in Italy and Germany--were treated to the increasingly absurd spectacle of royal uncles and cousins being maneuvered and married with farcical solemnity. The basis of political legitimacy in Europe was shifting. The principles of divine and aristocratic right were rapidly yielding to the principle of popular sovereignty--of the "will of the people" as the cornerstone of modern politics.

The tumult of 1848 brought home once again the rising demand for greater public participation in government. The pace of democratic reform quickened for the remainder of the century. Suffrage as expanded, parliaments spoke with increased authority, the secret ballot was introduced. The plebiscite returned to international prominence in the 1860s as an important part of the process that brought about the annexation of Savoy and Nice to France and the unification of Italy. Proposals for plebiscites became a regular feature of European diplomacy. Plebiscites were considered in Moldavia, Schleswig-Holstein, Heligoland, and Tacna-Arica. Plebiscites were carried out in the Ionian Islands, St. Bartholomew (Lesser Antilles), and the Danish West Indies (the Virgin Islands).

The attitude of the United States toward the plebiscite in the nineteenth century was an ambiguous one. President Jefferson, the great democrat of his era, purchased Louisiana from Napoleon without consulting the wishes of the inhabitants--although it could be reasonably presumed that the growing population of American settlers would have returned a large majority in favor of annexation. The U.S.A. backed the American settlers in Texas in their struggle to separate from Mexico, found an independent "Lone Star Republic," and then enter the Union.

Plebiscites were conducted in Texas, Tennessee, and

Virginia on the question of secession from the United States of America--secession winning by overwhelming majorities in all three states. These plebiscites were declared illegal by the U.S. government and were ultimately overturned by the victorious armies of the North. Approval was given, however, to a plebiscite that approved the secession of the western portion of Virginia from Virginia and the entry of the new state--West Virginia--into the Union.

In the eyes of much of the world, the Franco-Prussian War produced a serious violation of the principle of popular sovereignty. The uproar generated by the annexation of Alsace-Lorraine by Germany--conducted without the consultation of the inhabitants--underscored the unmistakable political reality of popular sovereignty. From the beginning of recorded history, territories and their people have been conquered, sold, or bartered. But now, in the second half of the nineteenth century, the denial of the right of national self-determination, for the first time, was proclaimed as a legitimate casus belli by one of the world's Great Powers: France. Henceforth, the principle of self-determination became mankind's chief rationale for warfare. The violation of the rights of the people of Belgium in 1914, of Poland in 1939, of South Vietnam in the 1960s, of the Falkland Islands in 1982 provided in the minds of many just cause for war.

THE PLEBISCITE IN THE POST-WORLD WAR ONE PERIOD

World War One, appropriately commenced by the act of a separatist assassin, ended with the destruction of two of the great adjacent empires--the Austro-Hungarian and the Ottoman Turkish. At the urging of President Woodrow Wilson, national self-determination for the subject peoples of Europe had become a principal "war aim" of the Allied and Associated Powers. The victors, amidst intense bargaining, proceeded to transform the map of Central and Eastern Europe. Demographic characteristics formed the basis for many of the new borders. But in many districts the ethnic composition of the population was mixed, patchy, or hotly disputed. Thus, plebiscites were conducted in a half dozen areas to ascertain the wishes of the inhabitants. These plebiscites are summarized below:

LOCATION	YEAR	NATIONALITIES	OUTCOME
Schleswig	1920	Danes, Germans	new border drawn
Allenstein and Marienwerder	1920	Germans, Poles	most awarded to Germany
Klagenfurt Basin	1920	Germans, Slovenes	awarded to Austria
Upper Silesia	1921	Germans, Poles	divided between Germany and Poland
Sopron	1921	Germans, Hungarians	awarded to Hungary
Saar	1935	Germans	awarded to Germany

Plebiscites were planned but not conducted in several areas:

LOCATION	YEAR	NATIONALITIES	OUTCOME
Teschen, Spisz, and Orava	1920	Czechs, Poles	settled by inter-state negotiation
Vilna	1920-21	Lithuanians, Poles	unresolved
Tacna and Arica	1925-26	Chileans, Peruvians	settled by inter-state negotiation

Thus, in the years following the First World War, the plebiscite received its most thorough testing as an instrument of conflict resolution. In the opinion of most neutral observers, the plebiscites worked remarkably well given the trauma of the war, the dislocated economies, the displaced populations, and the ferocious nationalisms of the time. In those areas of Europe where plebiscites were employed to determine sovereignty, the sources of rancor between states were largely removed. The plebiscites effectively defused six potential flashpoints--six sources of future inter-state discord--from the crowded agenda of European politics.

Perhaps it is a reflection of human nature that peacefully resolved disputes fade from memory quickly while festering disputes loom large in men's memories. Indeed, it was in territories that perhaps should have had plebiscites but where power politics prevailed--Danzig, the Sudetenland, Vilna, and, for fifteen years, the Saar--that the seeds of the Second World War took root.

An Example: The Schleswig Plebiscite, 1920

The first of the post-World War One plebiscites was contested in Schleswig. The Duchy of Schleswig together with its southern neighbor, the Duchy of Holstein, had been a sore spot on the map of northern Europe for nearly a century. Located in southern Jutland between the North Sea and the Baltic Sea, the region--often referred to as Schleswig-Holstein--had been held by the Danish kings since the Middle Ages. Holstein's population had become almost entirely German. By the early nineteenth century the southern districts of Schleswig were becoming progressively Germanized as well. Northern Schleswig, however, remained almost wholly Danish in character. By the mid-nineteenth century the German inhabitants of the two Duchies began to agitate for a partition of the area and called for a plebiscite to determine the precise location of a new Prussian-Danish frontier.

An inconclusive war fought in 1848 between Prussia and Denmark was followed by a decisive war in 1864 wherein Prussia captured both Schleswig and Holstein. A defeated Denmark ceded both duchies to the dual sovereignty of Prussia and Prussia's wartime ally, Austria.

In 1866 the Prussians, in turn, soundly defeated Austria and duly forced the Austrians to sign-over exclusive ownership of the duchies to Prussia. However, the text of the peace treaty contained the stipulation that "the population of the northern districts of Schleswig shall be ceded to Denmark if, by a free vote, they express a wish to be united to Denmark."[5] The Prussian regime ignored the stipulation and promptly annexed all of Schleswig-Holstein.

In the decades that followed, a rigorous campaign of Germanization was conducted against the Danish culture and language. Danish was banned in the schools and the courts. Outspoken Danish nationalists were deported to Denmark. Protests by the Danish Government were dismissed by Berlin as unwarranted interferences in German domestic affairs.

The German defeat in World War One provided a worrisome opportunity for Denmark to press its call for a plebiscite in Schleswig. It was worrisome in the sense that Denmark wished to avoid any appearance of pillaging a prostrate Germany in its hour of defeat. Hence, Denmark gently urged the victorious Allied and Associated Powers and the German Government to carry-out the terms of the 1866 Treaty. Berlin, fearing the virtual dismemberment of Germany at the hands of the French, the Poles, and other neighboring countries, readily agreed to the long-promised plebiscite. (Indeed, Germany, fearing dismemberment, suddenly developed a warm regard for the principle of national self-determination and demanded plebiscites in German territories marked for transfer to other states.)

Accordingly, Article 109 of the Treaty of Versailles provided for the evacuation of all German troops and officials from the Schleswig plebiscite area and ordained a plebiscite commission to assume control of the area for the purpose of conducting the vote. Thus, the Schleswig Commission, composed of commissioners from Britain, France, Norway, and Sweden, became the first international commission in history to conduct a plebiscite. First, the Commission created a new police force recruited from the plebiscite area, reorganized the schools and the civil service to eliminate discrimination against either Danes or Germans, and suspended or amended all existing laws or statutes that were seen as prejudicial to the rights of either community. Railroad, postal, telephone, and telegraph services were supervised to assure free access by inhabitants of the plebiscite area. Checkpoints were established to supervise entry and exit to the zone. Simultaneously, a list of qualified voters was prepared and published, election officials appointed and trained, rules to regulate the campaign devised, and Allied troops (on loan to the Commission) were deployed.

After a spirited campaign, the qualified voters cast their ballots either for cession to Denmark or to Germany. A turnout in excess of 90% was achieved. The Commission, after a close study of the pattern of voting, drew a new border between Denmark and Germany reflecting the predominant wishes of the inhabitants.

The new frontier, accepted by Denmark, Germany, and the international community, has stood the test of time. Thus, the plebiscite effectively removed the long-simmering "Schleswig-Holstein Question" from the list of international disputes.

THE PLEBISCITE IN THE POST-WORLD WAR TWO PERIOD

Unlike the first war, the second great war of the century was not fought by the Western Allies with national self-determination as an official war aim. Indeed, no new

European states emerged out of the war and several states (Estonia, Latvia, and Lithuania) lost their statehood. Unexpectedly and unintentionally, however, the war provided an enormous boost to nationalist movements outside of Europe. In Africa, the Middle East, and South Asia, nationalist groups that had shrewdly stood by their colonial masters during the war demanded recompense. Lebanon, Israel, the Philippines, Burma, India, Pakistan, and Libya formed the first cohort of what was to become a legion of newly independent states. Wars of national liberation erupted in Southeast Asia and in North Africa to lend additional impetus to the drive for decolonization.

Colonial territories taken from the defeated powers (Germany, Italy, and Japan) were placed under the supervision of the United Nations Trusteeship Council. The Trust Territories were administered by the Western powers (the United States, the United Kingdom, France) whose conduct was closely monitored by the Trusteeship Council. Unlike in the Mandate System of the League of Nations, trusteeship was defined explicitly as a transitional condition leading to independence. Thus, the Trusteeship Council was to guide the Trust Territories to independence and was then to bring down the curtain upon itself.

Following the lead of the League's Mandate System, the Trusteeship Council permitted individuals and groups living in the Trust Territories (or anyone in the world) to petition the Trusteeship Council. Hence, the centuries old maxim that only states possessed legal standing before international governmental organizations had been breached. The opening of this communication link with the residents of the Trust Territories enabled the Trusteeship Council to hold the Administering Powers more closely accountable for their behavior in a manner heretofore unprecedented.

EXAMPLES OF PETITIONS SUBMITTED TO THE UNITED NATIONS TRUSTEESHIP COUNCIL

DOCUMENT T/PET.GENERAL/13

Petition, transmitted by cablegram to the Secretary-General, dated 31 August 1947, from the Pro-Italy Association of War Veterans of Eritrea, Keren, Eritrea, concerning the operation of the International Trusteeship System in respect to Eritrea.

The Pro-Italy Association of War Veterans of Eritrea and families of deceased veterans meeting in an open assembly at Keren on 27 July 1947 adopted the following resolution: "The Directors of the Section of Eritrean Veterans and families of deceased veterans, mindful of the glorious, heroic tradition of the Eritrean Ascari, reassert their devoted attachment to the Italian flag. Desirous not only of guaranteeing the satisfaction of their own rights but also the true interests of the Eritrean people, they express the fervent hope that the Italian Government will soon assume the administration of this territory under the Trusteeship System and that, continuing the brilliant work of civil progress performed in the past, it (the Italian Government) will put Eritrea on the way to independence and self-government. In communicating to the Secretariat the hopes of the former Eritrean Ascari, we express our absolute confidence that the Big Four and the Council of the United Nations will fulfill the declarations of the San Francisco Charter in the matter of complying with the wishes of the Eritrean people as to the future political attribution of this territory.

Caffel Hassen-Bennabi
President, Pro-Italy Association
of War Veterans of Eritrea

DOCUMENT T/PET.2/31

Petition, dated 27 May 1947, from H. Arnesen, Moshi, Tanganyika.

P.O. Box 43
Moshi
Tanganyika Territory
East Africa
27 May 1947

The Secretary
United Nations
Washington
United States America

Sir,

I am born Norwegian and still a Norwegian subject. Have been living in Kenya Colony and Tanganyika Territory thirty-three years, the last twenty-five in Tanganyika. I have a clean record as I have never been in conflict with the law. Am a sawmiller by profession. During the 1939-1945 war I have been victimized by the Forest Dept. and Timber Control of the Territory and on account of this victimization have suffered losses amounting to several thousand pounds sterling.

Experience has shown that appeals to the Chief Secretary of Tanganyika Territory do not give satisfaction or fair play. I now beg to enquire whether your organization can institute an inquiry into my complaints in which case I will give further details supported by documents.

I am, Sir

Your obedient servant,

H. Arnesen

DOCUMENT T/PET.6/3-T/PET.7/4

Petition, dated 26 July 1947, from the All-Ewe Conference, concerning Togoland under British administration and Togoland under French administration.

P.O. Box 225
Accra
Gold Coast
26 July 1947

Trygve Lie, Esqr.
Secretary-General
United Nations
Lake Success
New York, U.S.A.

Sir,

I have the honour to forward to you herewith one original copy of the Ewe Convention of February, 1946.

One original copy of this Convention was previously sent to the United Nations Organization through the Honourable, The Colonial Secretary of the Gold Coast, as long ago as 3 June 1946. It now appears to us that that copy of the Convention never reached the United Nations Organization, and I am therefore posting to you the copy herewith enclosed.

I have the honour to be, Sir, your obedient servant,

E. Amu
General Secretary,
All-Ewe Conference

DOCUMENT T/PET.4/46

Petition from Mr. N.D. Fongum concerning the Cameroons under British administration.

N.D. Fongum, Widikum
29th October 1949

Through the D.O. Mamfe To the United Nation Ontour Mamfe

Sir,

I am here by laying the fowoling reports about my Village

A. The Widikum Store has no goods in it
B. The Widikum Mumo river has no good bridge which a lorry can cross on
C. No better court building

I have the honor to be, Sir,
Your obedient Servant,
N.D. Fongum of Widikum
Mamfe

The Trusteeship Council has supervised the conduct of a large number of referenda and several plebiscites in the Trust Territories. In so doing, the United Nations Trusteeship Council has developed vast expertise in the practical techniques of self-determination and has provided a model--often ignored--for the decolonization process.

AN EXAMPLE: THE PLEBISCITES IN THE UNITED NATIONS TRUST TERRITORY OF BRITISH CAMEROONS, 1959-1961

After nearly fifteen years of supervision by the United Nations Trusteeship Council, the British Cameroons, a fragment of land adjacent to the Republic of the Cameroons and the soon to be independent Federation of Nigeria, was deemed ready for self-determination. Visiting missions dispatched by the Trusteeship Council to the Trust Territory reported that the people of the northern districts appeared to favor joining with Nigeria while the southern districts seemed divided between uniting with Nigeria or with the Republic of the Cameroons. The Trusteeship Council voted to instruct Britain to conduct a series of plebiscites in the Territory under the supervision of a United Nations Plebiscite Commissioner. In the northern districts the issue was put thusly to the inhabitants:

> Do you wish Northern Cameroons to be a part of the Northern Region of Nigeria when the Federation of Nigeria becomes independent?
>
> or
>
> Are you in favor of deciding the future of the Northern Cameroons at a later date?

Sixty-two percent of those voting opted to defer a decision until a later date.

The inhabitants of the southern districts were queried thusly:

> Do you wish to achieve independence by joining the independent Federation of Nigeria?
>
> or
>
> Do you wish to achieve independence by joining the independent Republic of the Camerun?

Just over seventy percent of the electorate endorsed the Cameroons option. Subsequently, the southern districts of the Trust Territory were duly joined to the Republic of the Cameroons.

Returning to the north, a second plebiscite was conducted two years later in which the issue was the same as had been put in the south:

> Do you wish to achieve independence by joining the independent Federation of Nigeria?
>
> or
>
> Do you wish to achieve independence by joining the independent Republic of Camerun?

Nearly sixty percent voted for Nigeria. Thus, the northern districts of the Trust Territory entered the Nigerian Federation as Sardauna Province.[7]

INTERNATIONALLY SUPERVISED ELECTIONS

Inspired by the internationally recognized fairness and impartiality of the plebiscites conducted under the League and the United Nations, there has been a rapid growth during the post-war period in the number of internationally supervised elections. In order to insure the validity of domestic elections, teams of observers from neighboring states, allied states, or from international organizations may be invited to observe elections campaigns and to monitor the casting and counting of ballots.

A SAMPLE OF RECENT INTERNATIONALLY SUPERVISED ELECTIONS

COUNTRY	YEAR	TYPE OF OBSERVERS
Greece	1946	allied states
Dominican Republic	1966	allied states
South Vietnam	1967	allied states
Zimbabwe-Rhodesia	1980	Commonwealth
Uganda	1980	Commonwealth
El Salvador	1982	allied states

The value of independent outside observers in assuring fair elections varies directly with the actual independence of the observers. At worst, outside observers may share the same ideological blinkers as the regime conducting the election and merely serve to ratify a predetermined result. At best, outside observers can, by their visible presence and by their access to the world media, hold regimes to a high standard of electoral probity.

AN EXAMPLE: THE INTERNATIONALLY SUPERVISED ELECTION IN UGANDA, 1980

The 1970s were years of unsurpassed suffering for the people of Uganda. The brutal depredations of the Amin regime were followed by a bloody civil war during which Tanzanian troops intervened and President Amin was ousted. The country was in a state of economic and administrative collapse. High on the agenda of the new Tanzanian-backed regime was a restoration of political legitimacy. It was believed that a free and genuinely competitive general election for a new parliament was essential to restoring morale and to promote national reconciliation.

However, severe problems stood in the way of new elections. Firstly, many of the administrative and manpower resources needed to conduct an election had been swept away in the preceding decade of disorders. Secondly, trust in the capacity of government--any government--to conduct a genuinely fair election was extremely low. After a decade of Idi Amin, the people of Uganda realistically anticipated intimidation and fraud--not honest elections.

The government, after seeing the useful contribution of the Commonwealth Observer Group in the Zimbabwe-Rhodesia elections earlier that year, chose to invite the Commonwealth to dispatch another group of observers. After consultations with the Commonwealth Secretary-General and the member countries of the Commonwealth, the following terms of reference were agreed:

> The Observer Group will observe every relevant aspect of the organisation and conduct of the elections by the Electoral Commission in accordance with the law of Uganda relating to elections. Their functions will be to ascertain in their impartial judgement, whether, in the context of that law, the elections have been free and fair. In furtherance of this objective, it will be competent for the group to bring to the attention of the Electoral Commission or the Ugandan authorities from time to time such matters as they consider pertinent.[8]

Nine observers, headed by the distinguished diplomat E.M. Debrah of Ghana and supported by 61 assistants, arrived in Uganda within a month. Members of the Observer Group were deployed throughout the country and supplied with vehicles and aircraft to enable them to monitor the electoral process in most of the constituencies.

> We made our presence known to the people of Uganda through a series of radio, television and newspaper announcements and through special markings on our vehicles. Our telephone numbers were also widely advertised.
>
> Our doors were open to all. We received an incessant flow of visitors. In addition, we

made it a point during our travels to meet a wide and random cross-section of the people of Uganda of all political persuasions, as indeed we were free to do.

On the eve of the poll our Members were spread right across the country, strategically placed to be present at polling stations well before they were due to open. We were able to sample the poll in 92 of the 109 constituencies in which a contest was taking place,and in the course of doing so visited no fewer than 1476 polling stations, almost a third of the total. Between us we travelled a total of 62,100 miles, of which 41,900 were by road and 20,200 miles by air.[9]

The Observer Group carefully scrutinized the compilation of the electoral register to see that no voter was excluded unjustly. Particular note was made of the conduct of government officials, civil servants, police and army units to insure that no untoward influence was exerted during registration, the campaign, the balloting, and during the counting of the ballots. The media, especially the electronic media which was wholly controlled by the government, was monitored for fairness, i.e., did the candidates and parties each receive reasonably proportionate access?

The presence of the Observer Group appeared to reassure the candidates and the general public that they could campaign freely. Given the violence of the previous years of military dictatorship, intimidation of the voters during the campaign and at the polls was greatly feared.

In truth, we were surprised not that allegations of intimidation were being made but that they were, in the context of Uganda and our experience in some other countries, of such a limited character. Nevertheless, we judged it prudent to do all in our power to eliminate all possibility of intimidation becoming a grievance on polling day. Having personally witnessed the delays and occasional harassment of civilians at road blocks, and being conscious of their potential for abuse on polling day we urged the Chairman of the Military Commission to ensure that they were removed throughout the country on 10 December. It is gratifying that our

> suggestion was accepted. We also urged that all military personnel be confined to barracks on that day as we feared that their very presence in the vicinity of polling stations might be construed as being oppressive. Our suggestion in this respect was also accepted and acted upon. We have no doubt that these two decisions on the part of the Military Commission made an enormous contribution to the psychological climate in which polling took place.[10]

The Observer Group closely monitored the balloting on polling day. After the last ballots were cast, they supervised the sealing of the ballot boxes and accompanied them to the counting centers.

The Observer Group summed-up its observations in its official report:

> This has been a turbulent and troubled election, characterised by confusion, delays, intense mistrust, and in the end, a sense of wonder that it happened at all. Some, at least, of these difficulties could have been mitigated, even in Uganda's situation, if the Electoral Commission had been a more efficient and imaginative body than proved to be the case; if the Military Commission had not delayed a final decision and announcement on the venue and manner of the count till just three days before polling; if there had been a mechanism for continuing consultation between the Electoral Commission and all the political parties, sitting together, to consider and resolve difficulties as they arose; and if logistical arrangements for the distribution of balloting material had been made with a greater degree of thoroughness.
>
> We have expressed at some length our reservations regarding nominations and a number of the unopposed returns: without question, this is the area most open to criticism, but is one where the courts have the power to provide redress. We would, however, add that about half the seats involved are likely to have been captured by the UPC in any event, so that despite their effect on the arithmetic, they are unlikely to have affected the outcome.
>
> In the remainder of the country, despite

> all deficiencies, the electoral process cohered and held together even if some of its individual strands were frayed. Surmounting all obstacles, the people of Uganda, like some great tidal wave, carried the electoral process to a worthy and valid conclusion.[11]

CONCLUSION

The rise of the plebiscite as a tool of conflict resolution in matters concerning sovereignty has paralleled that of the principle of popular sovereignty. As the "will of the people" has grown to become the dominant source of political legitimacy for governments the world over, so too have democratically-based conflict resolution techniques such as the plebiscite grown in stature. Beginning as a technique exploited by the French revolutionaries to ratify their conquests, the plebiscite has developed into a serviceable tool to resolve disputes over sovereignty.

Nevertheless, the plebiscite remains something of an exotic creature. Given the lengthy catalogue of inter-state conflicts, bloody secessionist and irredentist struggles, and wars of national liberation, it is remarkable how few plebiscites--indeed, peaceful techniques of conflict resolution of all types--have been attempted. War remains in the eyes of much of mankind the great solvent, the righter of wrongs, the hammer of justice. The glory of war, the mystique of violence retains a powerful hold upon us. States, ever jealous of their monopoly over the waging of war and the making of peace, continue to prefer direct bilateral or multilateral negotiations between themselves--over the heads of the peoples immediately involved. To submit a dispute to a court, to an arbitrator, or to the verdict of the affected electorate means a loss of state control. Thus, the club of states continues to regard the plebiscite with suspicion, employing it only when other techniques are either unavailable or too costly.

Contributing to the neglect of the plebiscite by states is a widespread ignorance about the technique. Given its infrequent use in the past, both statesmen and citizens share a lack of practical contact with the plebiscite technique. Few are aware of the conditions in which a plebiscite can be appropriate. Fewer still are conversant with the large corpus of practical experience developed by trial and error in plebiscites and internationally supervised elections during the past century.

NOTES

[1]Cornelius Tacitus, The Germania and the Agricola (London: Penguin Books, 1955).

[2]Johannes Mattern, The Employment of the Plebiscite in the Determination of Sovereignty (Baltimore: The Johns Hopkins Press, 1920), p. 44.

[3]The Declaration of Independence, signed in Philadelphia on July 4, 1776.

[4]Mattern, p. 65.

[5]Sarah Wambaugh, Plebiscites Since the World War (Washington, D.C.: Carnegie Endowment for International Peace, 1933), p. 49-50.

[6]The responses to these petitions are also available in the records of the Trusteeship Council.

[7]U.O Umozurike, Self-Determination in International Law (Hamden: Archon Books, 1972), pp. 105-106.

[8]Uganda Elections: December 1980. The Report of the Commonwealth Observer Group (London: Commonwealth Secretariat, 1980), p. 5.

[9]Uganda Elections, p. 7.

[10]Uganda Elections, p. 21.

[11]Uganda Elections, p. 32.

3

The Mechanics of a Plebiscite

The credibility of a plebiscite lies in its procedural mechanics. Most of the nineteenth century plebiscites were procedurally flawed. Discussing the Lombardy plebiscite, Bolton King notes:

> Later experience has shown how untrustworthy a plebiscite may be, how with a people untrained in political life a vote on a single issue, taken hurriedly without free and full discussion may be far from representing the real feelings of a people. . . The republicans, divided and irresolute . . . for the most part abstained. Villagers voted under the eyes of the priest, soldiers at their officers' bidding; forgery, pressure, coercion were freely used.[1]

A defective plebiscite delivers a defective title to sovereignty. Because the plebiscite technique is rooted in the bedrock of our era's concept of political legitimacy--the will of the people--any ingenuous or fraudulent use of it aggravates and magnifies the political conflicts plebiscites are meant to help resolve.

Recent decades have provided ample testimony to the ease with which electoral mechanisms can be adapted to serve the needs of dictators. Indeed, there are few things easier to debauch than a free election. While the "will of the people" has become the source of legitimacy, the mechanism to permit the vigorous expression of the people's will--a free, competitive election--is far from being firmly established in much of the world.

Few states are so impolite as to make an issue of the

electoral procedures of other states. States seek to continue "business as usual" with other states and elections--free or fraudulent--appear to have little effect upon global patterns of aid, trade, and alliance.

In light of this attitude, it is remarkable that when a people are permitted to participate in a plebiscite, the world community demands that it be impeccably fair and free. Exacting standards have been demanded for the plebiscites conducted in the United Nations Trust Territories, for the Zimbabwe-Rhodesia vote, and for the proposed United Nations supervised elections in Namibia-South-West Africa. It would be wrong to dismiss such demands for open, competitive elections as pure hypocrisy. There is the pragmatic recognition by states that a fair and free plebiscite can contribute to the resolution of costly and dangerous conflicts--conflicts that may destabilize whole regions or bring the threat of war to the doorstep. A genuinely free election is also a safeguard against the hazard of more resourceful or better positioned states "stealing" the election through fraud or intimidation.

The freeness and fairness of an election is a matter of procedures--procedures that are open and impartial, procedures that demonstrably encourage and protect free speech and permit a vigorous campaign, procedures that guarantee a secret and accurately counted poll. Every step of a plebiscite from beginning to end is subject to the intensive scrutiny of a suspicious world community. Thus, it must reflect the global "state of the art" of election management. Yet, as Rokkan declares:

> Given the crucial importance of the organization of legitimate elections in the development of the mass democracies of the twentieth century, it is indeed astounding to discover how little serious effort has been invested in the comparative study of the wealth of information available. . . The great bulk of the items bear on technicalities and controversies within a single national or regional tradition, and the few wider-ranging ones tend to take the form of vehement polemics against competing systems, even when couched in the terms of academic discourse.[2]

Since there is no globally recognized technology of free elections, plebiscites must embody the highest denominator of free electoral practices in current use. It is a high standard but one that is capable of attainment--as demonstrated by the successful plebiscites of this century. The attainment of such a standard requires, in the words of Baker, what appear to be "ludicrously detailed procedures."[3] This is because the procedures must be sufficiently thorough and rigorous to persuade both the inhabitants of a plebiscite zone and the world community of the fairness of the electoral process. If this is accomplished, the verdict is likely to be sustained.

The following pages will survey in detail the complex and often fascinating mechanics of conducting a plebiscite. It is a guide based upon the lessons learned in the plebiscites and internationally supervised elections of the past century. It is an exploration into the technology of democracy.

AGREEMENT BETWEEN THE PARTIES INVOLVED

Plebiscites emerge out of the on-going process of diplomatic bargaining in much the same fashion as ceasefires, alliances, arbitration panels, wars, economic sanctions, and international organizations. At a point of flux, where the matrix of costs and benefits has shifted for the state and non-state parties to a sovereignty dispute, a plebiscite may become a feasible option. Generally speaking, states prefer other methods of settlement--methods that involve direct negotiation between states and that do not risk the uncertainty brought about when non-state parties are participants. States lose control when international courts, arbitration panels, or plebiscites are employed. Thus, plebiscites--like the other techniques of peaceful third party settlement--tend to be used (1) after the big issues have been resolved by the states (often by war) or (2) when an increasingly costly dispute proves resistant to resolution by direct negotiations or (3) when non-state actors have so forcibly intruded into matters that new sovereignty arrangements are all but inevitable. In an era such as ours when wars between states and non-state groups number in the dozens, opportunities for the use of the plebiscite technique have never been greater.

INITIAL SURVEY

The first tangible step toward the holding of a plebiscite is the creation of a small research commission to conduct an initial survey of the prospects for a plebiscite. The research commission, while studying the lessons of previous plebiscites, should proceed to the prospective plebiscite zone and undertake immediately the following tasks: locate and secure essential records; assess the impartiality of the local civil administration and police force; develop preliminary estimates of the number, size, density, and dispersion of ethnic, linguistic, religious, and economic groups in the zone; assess the prospects for the withdrawal of all troops from the zone (or to bases and assembly areas) and develop estimates of the minimum size of a neutral observer force; assess the impact of "new facts" established in the zone by the state(s) presently occupying it and estimate the extent to which any "new facts" could be neutralized in the event of a plebiscite; assess whether the plebiscite should decide the fate of the zone as a whole or of each district--with a view to possible partition; estimate the time that will be required to install a plebiscite regime, to neutralize the local civil and police administration, to establish a plebiscitary atmosphere, to conduct the vote, and to implement the traditional steps necessary to deliver the zone to its newly chosen sovereignty(s).

Locate and Secure Records

The most immediate task of the research commission is the locating and safeguarding of local records that will be needed for the plebiscite. A complete data base is essential for the creation at a later time of lists of eligible voters. Detailed records are also needed for the identification and certification of outvoters and refugees and for the effective supervision of civil and police authorities under a future plebiscite regime.

There exists a genuine danger that key records may be altered or destroyed by those seeking to disrupt or block the conduct of a plebiscite. In the Saar a "Provisional Records Commissioner" was appointed in 1922 to locate, classify, and secure the documents needed for the plebiscite.[4] The Commissioner, Dr. Alfred Bonzon, in his first official report, listed the documents he had secured in order of importance:

census returns
tax records
police registers of arrivals and departures
card indices for all inhabitants
registry office documents
voters lists
records used for the rationing of food and coal
military recruiting registers

Each research commission must determine which of the existing local records in the future plebiscite zone would be useful to the conduct of the plebiscite.

Finally, a survey must be made of those records normally kept outside the potential plebiscite zone and which may prove essential to the work of a plebiscite regime. Enquiries should be made concerning the availability of such records and, if possible, assurances obtained (in writing) of their future availability.

Impartiality of Local Administration

An assessment must be made of the impartiality and professionalism of the local civil administration and police force. If they are highly politicized and firmly in the camp of one of the potential parties to the plebiscite, judgments must be made concerning the manner in which they may be neutralized under a plebiscite regime.

Demographic Estimate

Data must be collected on the ethnic, linguistic,religious, and economic patterns of the population in the area. This information may prove decisive when the boundaries of the plebiscite zone are drawn and the voting districts within the zone are formulated. Hard data for some of the variables may be unobtainable. Available data must be carefully scrutinized since data concerning ethnic minority groups is notoriously inaccurate in most countries.

Withdrawal of Troops

If the potential plebiscite area is at peace, the withdrawal of troops for the purpose of the plebiscite can be handled routinely. If the area is a war zone, an assessment must be made of the number and type of soldiers--both government and insurgent--operating in the area. The main operational areas and bases should be pinpointed. An estimate must be made of the size, type, and likely deployment pattern of neutral troops that will be used to secure the area following the withdrawal.

New Facts

Perhaps the most vexing obstacle that may stand in the way of a plebiscite is the problem of "new facts." New facts are the product of intentional changes made by states in the demographic character of an area. In 1919 the French argued that a plebiscite in Alsace-Lorraine would be unjust after nearly fifty years of brutal German suppression of French culture, large-scale German colonization, and the emigration of nearly half a million French-speakers from Alsace-Lorraine since 1871. These "new facts," created with premeditation by the German Government, made a plebiscite in 1919 utterly unacceptable to France. The plebiscite, they insisted, should have been held in 1871. Needless to say, Alsace and Lorraine were annexed forthwith by a triumphant France under the terms of the Treaty of Versailles and no plebiscite was conducted.

A contemporary example of the problem of "new facts" may be seen in Israeli policy in the West Bank of the Jordan. Beginning with the capture of the territory in 1967, the Israeli State has pursued a policy of planting Jewish settlements throughout the West Bank with the express purpose of altering the demographic pattern. Ultimately, there will be a sufficient number of Israeli voters and business interests located in the West Bank to negate the possibility of yielding the territory at the bargaining table. By the early 1980s some Arabs were predicting that Israel would carry the "new facts" policy to its logical conclusion and expel--under some pretext--hundreds of thousands of Palestinians from the West Bank. Israel would thereby achieve a Jewish majority much as was done in Israel proper in 1948. Israel would then presumably welcome a plebiscite. The Palestinians would say, as they do now, that the only legitimate date for a plebiscite would have been prior to 1948 and conducted in the entire Palestine Mandate. A plebiscite today would be acceptable to the Palestinians if Palestinian refugees throughout the world would be allowed to participate as outvoters.

A brief summary of any "new facts" in a potential

plebiscite area must be made by the research commission. The extent and the dates of colonization, if any, must be ascertained. The number and current countries of residence of emigrants and expellees must be estimated since these people are likely outvoters in any plebiscite. The patterns of economic dependence within the zone and between the zone and neighboring states must be assessed.

Many "new facts" cannot and often, perhaps, should not be reversed. Nevertheless, they can be factored into a formula that balances historical facts with the rights of today's citizens to determine their future. Examples of such formulae are commonplace in domestic political life. The United States' Constitution reflects the historical fact that some of the states that formed the early American federation were large in population and some small. Hence, the Senate (with two senators for each state) reflects this continuing historical fact while the House of Representatives (the number of representatives proportionate to the population of each state) reflects the "one man, one vote" principle of majoritarian government.

Whole or Parts

If an area is a coherent ethnic,economic,and geographic whole, such as the Saar, any plebiscite to determine sovereignty over the area should treat the area as a single entity. If as is more commonly the case, the area is fragmented, the plebiscite vote should be recorded in many small districts. The distribution of the vote in the districts can then be used, as was done in Schleswig and Upper Silesia, to partition the area.

Time Frame

The final task of the research commission is to estimate the time that would be required for each of the phases of a plebiscite: the installation of the plebiscite regime, the neutralization of the local civil administration and police force, the establishment of a plebiscitary atmosphere, the conduct of the vote, the implementation of the electorate's decision. The most difficult of the time estimates is that regarding the establishment of a plebiscitary atmosphere. Such a phase could take weeks, months, or years. It is in this phase that attempted plebiscites are most likely to fail. As in Vilna and Tacna-Arica, an atmosphere of intimidation and fear can destroy the very basis of a plebiscite. Careful study of the successes and failures of previous plebiscite regimes to create the necessary atmosphere for a valid poll can prove most valuable to the formulation of this estimate.

PLEBISCITE CONFERENCE

If the state and non-state parties to a sovereignty dispute view the prospects for a plebiscite as favorable, the next step is the calling of a Plebiscite Conference to lay down the structure and parameters of the plebiscite. History provides many formulae for representation at such conferences wherein non-state parties sit as members of certain state delegations or are granted official observer status.

The first task of the Conference is to frame the question(s) to be decided by the plebiscite. Is it a choice of which neighboring state the people of an area wish to join? Is the choice between affiliation with an existing state or with a to-be-created sovereign state? A study of diplomatic history will show that a wide variety of permutations are available at this stage. Nevertheless, it is essential that the parties to the Conference know what issue the plebiscite will decide and commit themselves in advance to accepting any of the range of outcomes that they have outlined.

POSSIBLE OUTCOMES: FRAMING THE QUESTION

OUTCOME	ILLUSTRATION
No Change	Saar (1955)
Partition between States	Schleswig (1920)
Partition between Existing State and New State(s)	Upper Silesia (1920)
Condominium	New Hebrides (1906-1980)
New State	Norway (1905)
Local Autonomy	Jura (1978)
Commonwealth Status	Puerto Rico (1967)
Federation with Existing State	British Cameroons (1959)
Consociational Federation	None
International Regime	Tangier (1923-1956)
International Regime followed by Plebiscite	Saar (1920-1935)
U.N. Trusteeship	U.N. Trust Territories

The next major task for the Conference is to define the boundaries of the plebiscite zone and to determine who will be eligible to vote. The latter issue may prove complex if there are recent settlers in the zone or if there are large numbers of refugees or emigrants from the zone. (Both the issue of boundaries and of voter qualification will be discussed in detail later.)

The remainder of a typical agenda for a Plebiscite Conference should look as follows:

1. Create and empower a Plebiscite Commission to organize and conduct the plebiscite.
2. Appoint the members of the Plebiscite Commission and confer upon them (and anyone they, in turn, should appoint) the privileges and immunities of diplomatic rank.
3. Approve the method of financing the costs of the plebiscite.
4. Establish a plan and timetable for the withdrawal of troops from the plebiscite zone.
5. Organize and dispatch a contingent of neutral troops to the zone.
6. Formulate plans for the repatriation of refugees, exiles, and deportees.
7. Agree to a formula for the settlement of state assets in the plebiscite zone should sovereignty be transferred.
8. Establish appropriate reciprocity agreements to guarantee the existing pension and social insurance entitlements of the zone's inhabitants.
9. Execute a pledge by all parties to the Conference that no reprisals will be taken against any person in the plebiscite zone for opinions expressed or legal political acts undertaken as part of the plebiscite.
10. If possible, record promises of economic aid and other benefits for the people of the plebiscite zone--aid to be provided irrespective of the ultimate outcome of the vote.

Having created the institutions of the plebiscite and having prepared the necessary ground, the Plebiscite Conference may adjourn to await the report of the Plebiscite Commission following the conduct of the plebiscite vote.

PLEBISCITE COMMISSION

A Plebiscite Commission has two paramount tasks: The conduct of the plebiscite itself and the administration of the plebiscite zone before and immediately after the vote. It is, in essence, a caretaker government for the area designated for the plebiscite. It is imperative that the Commission be fully empowered to undertake both tasks--not just the conduct of the vote alone.[5] As will be developed later, the Plebiscite Commission must have the authority to neutralize as completely as possible the local civil administration, the courts, and especially, the police force.

Powers

The powers of a Plebiscite Commission derive from the agreement reached earlier by the principal state and non-state parties to the Plebiscite Conference. Its powers will reflect the bargain struck by these parties. The grant of power may be either plenipotentiary or delegative. Plenipotentiary power is a broad grant of authority to accomplish specific tasks (e.g., administer the zone and conduct the vote) which leaves the Commission free to interpret its own powers in any manner not inconsistent with the initial grant. Delegative power is a limited grant of authority to undertake specified tasks under the supervision of a superior body, i.e., the Plebiscite Conference. With only delegative powers, for instance, a Plebiscite Commission's draft rules and regulations for a plebiscite would first be submitted to the Conference for approval.

It is not impossible for a Plebiscite Commission to fulfill its mission with delegative power--but it is highly unlikely. Firstly, an important element of a Plebiscite Commission's credibility with the inhabitants of a plebiscite zone is its palpable neutrality and independence. A Commission that must bargain--tacitly or openly--with a Conference of emphatically partisan actors is unlikely to appear impartial. The result is likely to be the unhappy fate suffered by the Kashmir plebiscite commission that found itself trapped between the partisans above--the states of the United Nations--and the partisans below--the divided people of Kashmir.[6] Secondly, given the short time frame for most plebiscites--a few months to a year--a Commission must be able to move expeditiously. The state and non-state parties to the Conference, for tactical reasons, invariably wish to advance or delay the date of the vote. Without the ability to control the pace of events inside the plebiscite zone, the Commission is likely to founder.

Most successful Plebiscite Commissions have been granted plenipotentiary power. They are thus free to administer the zone impartially, conduct the vote, and to report the result--together with recommendations concerning the result--to the Conference.

Composition of the Plebiscite Commission

The ideal members of a plebiscite commission would be persons of great stature and wide experience from neutral countries who are fully acquainted with the peoples and problems of the plebiscite zone and yet are personally impartial and disinterested on the issue of sovereignty in the zone. In practice, the members tend to be a mix of diplomats, retired government officials, and experienced academics from states outside the immediate vicinity of the plebiscite zone. It is usually best to fill the commission with as many neutrals as possible. Attempts to "balance" commissions with partisans from the various parties to the plebiscite have shown poor results. Wambaugh has concluded:

> We have found that a balance of partisans on a commission secures only an approximate and unstable form of neutrality and opens the door to constant friction. The presence of neutrals, on the other hand, on the Schleswig Commission gave it a character of neutrality lacking in the other commissions. We should carry this lesson further and provide that all members of the commission shall come from states sufficiently remote from the controversy to have no choice between the contenders. Moreover, such detachment must not only be real in fact but must be fully recognized as such.[7]

It is also useful for the Conference to appoint individuals to serve in their individual capacities rather than as representatives of states. This has two advantages. First, it underlines the independence and impartiality of the commissioners. Secondly, it may avoid the spectacle of states jockeying for seats on the commission and the resulting pressure for a "balance" among the various partisans.

Order of Business

The first order of business for a newly appointed plebiscite commission is the preparation of its own rules of procedure. Second comes the naming of assistants and technical advisors. Third, a rough division of labor among the commissioners is needed in which each takes responsibility for a segment of the local civil administration, e.g., one commissioner may supervise the courts and the police, another the bureaus of finance and revenue, another the postal, telephone, and telegraph services, etc.

Often, as the commission gets down to work, a strong spirit of teamwork develops among the commissioners. Even the United Nations Commission for India and Pakistan, which ultimately failed in its mission to hold a plebiscite in Kashmir, developed such a spirit:

> Step by step an atmosphere of complete mutual confidence developed among its members. Unhampered by the burden of power politics, refusing to apply in the Kashmir dispute the East-West rift which had so often poisoned the work of the United Nations in other cases, it proceeded as one body. The delegates lived mostly in the same hotels, and if the official proceedings indicated meetings of three or four hours' length, the fact is that the Kashmir dispute was on the agenda from morning till late at night: at breakfast, lunch, and dinner. The delegates became emotionally attached to the cause of Kashmir as if it were their own cause. I had attended many international conferences, but I had never witnessed anything like this.[8]

Finance

The normal operations of local government in a plebiscite zone are typically financed as much as possible from normal local tax revenues. If the local tax base is inadequate or has been damaged by war, the Conference participants must agree to underwrite any additional sums. In some plebiscites, where two states are contesting lands lying between them, the two states have agreed to split the cost. Germany and Denmark entered into such an agreement concerning the Schleswig plebiscite. (A novel--and self-enforcing--approach to financing such a plebiscite is for the winner to pick up the tab for the entire cost.) Often, large states with an interest in a peaceful resolution to an area's problems will provide or guarantee the necessary funds to ensure a smoothly conducted plebiscite.

NEUTRALIZING ADMINISTRATION

Civil Administration

The local civil administration in a plebiscite zone must be placed under the rigorous control of the plebiscite regime and completely removed from involvement in the politics of the plebiscite. Given the wide range of services and enforcement activities of most contemporary governments, civil servants are in a good position to use their power for partisan ends. Thus, it is especially important that bureaus with politically sensitive tasks be supervised closely. Failure to control even the mundane bureaus can have disruptive effects. This was clearly seen in Zimbabwe-Rhodesia (1980) where the newly appointed British Governor inherited a partisan, White-dominated civil administration resolutely hostile to the Black parties.

> When we arrived we found that the provision of telephones for the election offices both of the PF and ZANU (PF) had been the subject of protracted delay, which continued for a considerable time after our arrival and, in the case of ZANU (PF), the connections were not made until two weeks before polling day. Similarly, goods were held up in customs, and the PF and ZANU (PF) even encountered difficulty in obtaining maps, apparently on the grounds of "national security!" We are prepared to accept that in some instances at least, these parties had contributed to their difficulties by a lack of familiarity with the procedures laid down, but our impression was that at times the Administration was lethargic to the point of being obstructive. That it should have been so in comparatively minor matters lent credence to allegations of more serious bias.[9]

Neutral Inspectors

The most important technique used to neutralize the civil administration is the appointment by the Plebiscite Commission of neutral inspectors to oversee the operation of each bureau of local government. The inspectors should have full access to all the records and correspondence of their respective bureaus. All actions that previously required the signatures of a bureau director must be cosigned by an inspector. An inspector may recommend to the Commission changes in the rules and procedures of his bureau. Uncooperative or obstructive officials may be suspended from duty by order of an inspector. A code of conduct should be composed specifying dos and don'ts for the civil servants. Such codes tend to be well received because they indicate specific behaviors to be avoided and provide affirmative standards of conduct for civil servants who would otherwise be bewildered and unsure of themselves.

Sever Links

The chain of command linking the local administration with the central organs of any antecedent states must be cut. The Plebiscite Commission and its agents, the administrative inspectors, must become the masters of the local administration. All communication and correspondence with a bureau's superiors in the antecedent state(s) must be approved by an inspector. Members of the civil service--especially high ranking members--who are not residents of the plebiscite zone should be carefully screened and, where possible, replaced by local inhabitants.

Care should be taken not to sever permanently relationships to the bureaucracies of the antecedent state(s)--since the verdict of the plebiscite could produce reunification with those states. Reasonable guarantees of security of tenure for the civil servants of the plebiscite zone should be included in the initial agreement between the state and non-state parties at the Plebiscite Conference. Solid liaison should thus be maintained between the local civil service--under the supervision of neutral inspectors--and the bureaucracies of the antecedent state(s).

Special Ombudsman

Given the short time frame and the politically overheated atmosphere of most plebiscites, it is important that complaints lodged against the civil administration are handled quickly and impartially. A well-publicized and streamlined complaints procedure under the control of a special ombudsman can serve to curb any excesses of the civil administration and to reassure the public.

Local Advisory Boards

If the state of local political tension permits, joint advisory boards composed of local notables representing the parties to the plebiscite may be appointed. It has proven useful to place certain local elected officials onto these boards to provide them a means of making an input into the plebiscite process. Given that the personnel of the plebiscite regime is composed mostly of foreigners, local advisory groups can provide useful local expertise--steering the plebiscite regime away from hidden pitfalls. By playing a watchdog role, advisory groups can also play a useful part in the neutralization of the civil administration.

The Election Council in Zimbabwe-Rhodesia (1980) was a good illustration of the value of local advisory boards:

> The Election Council proved a most useful forum. Under skillful chairmanship, and with each party represented by two senior officials, the meetings demonstrated an encouraging ability on the part of all the parties to work together, and to achieve reasoned decisions in a very short time. Arrangements were made for us [the Commonwealth Observer Group] to be at its meetings, and we greatly benefited from our regular attendance.
>
> The Election Council was consulted on a wide variety of matters concerning all aspects of the elections. Discussions were brief and to the point, and little time was devoted to the scoring of political points. In addition, it provided a vehicle through which complaints

could be made, and frequently were, concerning aspects of the election arrangements and the election campaign which were troubling individual parties.[10]

Schools

Schools are vehicles of culture--not of culture per se but of specific cultures. The political power of dominant national groups is made manifest in the schools. Everything from the language of instruction to the version of history taught reflects the pattern of cultural dominance. Dissident national groups often view the schoolmaster--even more than the policeman--as the instrument of their oppression.

It is difficult for a plebiscite regime to do much about the educational system it inherits from the antecedent state(s). At best, certain gross forms of discrimination against the children of minority or dissident groups can be ended. For example, in German-controlled Upper Silesia it had been a punishable offense for students to speak in Polish--even outside of class. All instruction and examinations were in German. While the plebiscite regime could do little to correct the overwhelming bias in favor of Germans, it did proclaim Polish to be an official language of instruction and removed all penalities for its use. Polish-speaking teachers were recruited to provide at least a few hours a week of Polish language instruction to the Polish students. In Allenstein, where a similar pro-German bias existed, over twenty schoolmasters were sacked for violating the code of impartiality imposed on all public employees.[11]

In sum, unless the plebiscite period runs for a number of years, only important symbolic changes can be made to neutralize the schools. By doing so, the plebiscite regime communicates to the inhabitants of the plebiscite zone a sympathetic awareness of the linkage between education and national identity.

State-Owned and Multi-National Industries

Imagine a small coastal region in which the largest single employer is, say, a state-owned naval shipyard. The region becomes part of a plebiscite zone in which the inhabitants have the choice of separating from the state that owns the yard--and buys all the ships built by the yard. The government of the state broadly hints it will close the yard unless the people of the zone vote to rejoin the state.

People vote their economic interests as well as their national interests. Hence, they can be influenced by the carrots and sticks offered them by state-owned and privately-owned enterprises. There is little a plebiscite regime can do in this regard. Early in the plebiscite process agreements should be sought with large state-owned and multi-national corporate enterprises in which assurances are given not to contrive dramatic threats or promises during the plebiscite campaign. It is, of course, realistic for the people of a plebiscite zone to recognize that businesses regularly reassess their profitability and that the outcome of the plebiscite could have a bearing on such reassessments. However, the point should also be made that plebiscites (and the new, popularly approved sovereignty arrangements they produce) promise stability for peoples who have been beset by conflict. By removing uncertainty and, often, the clouds of war from an area, a plebiscite can usher in a new era of stable prosperity--a climate that attracts investment.

Churches

Churches the world over seem to have adjusted well to the explosive growth of nationalism in recent centuries. Often, the church becomes the virtual embodiment of national consciousness--as in Poland and Iran today. Large churches tend to organize their sees, dioceses, or synods in keeping with both state and national boundaries.

A politicized clergy can create serious problems for a plebiscite. Rumors of Polish priests refusing absolution to parishioners for the "sin" of voting for Germany inflamed passions in the Upper Silesia plebiscite. The bishops of Germany signed a declaration that all but ordered church members to vote for immediate reunification of the Saar with Germany in the 1935 plebiscite:

> On Sunday, January 13, there will be a plebiscite in the Saar Territory on the question whether this German land and its people shall remain under the separation from the German Reich imposed on them by the Versailles Peace of Force. To the momentous decision to be made in a few days in the Saar, which is fraught with such fateful consequences for the future of our Fatherland, no true German can remain

> indifferent. As German Catholics we have the duty to throw all our strength into work for the greatness, welfare, and peace of our Fatherland. Our most effective help is prayer. We therefore order that on the said Sunday in all churches, after the general prayer, three Our Fathers and three Ave Marias shall be recited with the congregation in order to entreat an issue of the Saar plebiscite beneficent to our German people.[12]

The usual approach taken to this problem by plebiscite regimes is to request church authorities to (a) detach the plebiscite zone from existing dioceses or church districts and (b) order the clergy in the zone to refrain from partisan pronouncements. Both of these steps were taken by the Vatican in connection with the plebiscites in Upper Silesia, Allenstein, and Marienwerder.

COURTS

It is essential that the existing court system of a plebiscite zone be neutralized thoroughly and visibly. A court is a living symbol of the authority of the state. While a court may be impartial in its application of the law to the citizenry, it is not impartial in terms of its relationship between the citizen and the state. It is the creature of the state--a part of the apparatus of coercion that includes the police and the prisons. Wambaugh reminds us:

> To expect the courts of one country at all times to give justice to the party wishing to escape from its jurisdiction is asking too much of human nature, just as it is too much to expect the people in subjection to believe that they will receive justice from the courts of their rulers while engaged in a campaign to end that rule.[13]

New Appellate Courts

The first step in the neutralization of a court system is the severing of its connection to all higher courts outside the plebiscite zone. Then, a new appellate court must be created by the Plebiscite Commission. Given the temporary character of such appellate courts and the need for unquestioned impartiality, it is usually best to appoint distinguished jurists or law professors from neutral countries to serve as judges. Alternatively, local notables representing the national groups contesting the plebiscite may be appointed under the supervision of a chief judge brought-in from a neutral country. This approach is particularly useful in circumstances where one national group has dominated the legal system to the detriment of others. For example, in Marienwerder two Poles were appointed to the new court--the first time Poles had been permitted to serve as judges.[14] Thus, the Polish community could see their own leaders taking part in the legal system. As a means of building the confidence of the long repressed Polish inhabitants, the naming of Polish as well as German judges to the new court was more effective than the appointment of a panel of judges from neutral countries.

Vet Existing Judges

Again, given the temporary nature of a plebiscite regime, the existing courts of original jurisdiction are normally retained intact. However, the sitting judges must normally be screened; removing those with strong political ties to the parties contesting the plebiscite and those who have become notorious in their past judicial treatment of particular groups or races.[15]

The position of the judges that survive the vetting process is one of considerable sensitivity. They have a legitimate fear for their careers--not to mention their pensions--if the verdict of the plebiscite goes against the state which previously controlled the area. Even if the previous sovereignty is restored, they may be tainted by their collaboration with the plebiscite regime. Thus, either all of the sitting judges should be removed (a sure source of unrest and a move likely to immobilize the court system) or those that are retained should be protected in two ways. First, no oath of loyalty to the plebiscite regime should be required--only an oath promising to uphold the law in a fair and impartial manner. Secondly, as part of the original agreement between the several states and communities involved in the plebiscite, a specific pledge of no reprisals against all officials in the plebiscite zone (judges, police, civil servants) must be made.

Supervise Sitting Judges

A new appellate court or a separate review panel should monitor the behavior of the lower court judges. Judges not meeting a reasonable standard of conscientious impartiality may be suspended or removed by the reviewing body. It is essential that the reviewing body itself be regarded by the local legal community as impartial and non-partisan. If this is not so, the legal system is likely to break down as indeed happened in Upper Silesia when the German judges went out on strike and the Plebiscite Commission was unable to conscript local Germans to replace them.[16]

Review Existing Law

Most plebiscitary regimes retain the pre-existing corpus of statutes. However, the statute books are normally subjected to a thorough review. Laws which would hinder or obstruct the conduct of the plebiscite or the authority of the plebiscite regime are removed or amended. Laws that have the effect of discriminating against one or more of the groups contesting the plebiscite must be identified and altered. This is not always an easy task since decades of legal practice can subtly change the import of a rule to work in favor of some groups and against others.

Decisions of higher courts located outside the plebiscite zone that remain in force must also be assessed. For instance, a high court order to suspend a dissident newspaper for two years would require review if the two year period was still in effect.

Agreement to Assimilate Verdicts

The initial agreement between the state and non-state actors establishing the plebiscite mechanism should include a pledge that any state or states assuming sovereignty over the plebiscite area in the future will endeavor to assimilate the verdicts reached by the plebiscite regime's courts. Such an agreement both heightens the credibility of the courts prior to the plebiscite vote and smooths what can often be an awkward transfer of sovereignty later. In practice, the "winners" of plebiscites have proven most magnanimous in the past on the issue of assimilating verdicts. Even governments bitterly critical of the plebiscite regime and its courts before the vote--such as the Nazi German government in

1935--tend upon winning to praise and accept the validity of the plebiscite process. (Clearly, the more valid the plebiscite, the more valid the winner's claim to sovereignty over the once disputed territory.)

Three Amnesties

The sentences meted out to prisoners by the antecedent state's courts must be reviewed by the plebiscite regime. Often, a general amnesty is declared for those imprisoned for political causes. Typically, prisoners incarcerated for non-political offenses are permitted to apply for amnesty if they claim that political motives lay behind their convictions.

A second kind of amnesty that has been useful in creating a plebiscitary atmosphere has been the amnesty that bars prosecution for politically motivated offenses committed before the plebiscite period. One of Lord Soames' first acts upon becoming the new Royal Governor of Southern Rhodesia in December 1979 was to enact an Amnesty Ordinance which absolved from criminal liability those who had committed acts of treason against the Crown (most White Rhodesians who supported the Unilateral Declaration of Independence in 1965) and those who had waged war against the independent Rhodesian regime (many Black Rhodesians involved in the guerrilla war).[17]

A third kind of amnesty comes after the plebiscite is conducted. With the exception of those persons charged or convicted for crimes of violence or for actions aimed at undermining the integrity of the plebiscite vote itself, charges are dropped and punishments are terminated. For example, the Schleswig Commission in 1920 declared such an amnesty the day following the vote. Plebiscites often generate strong emotions and rash acts are committed in the heat of the moment. Properly timed amnesties can contribute significantly to the calming of the transitional period that follows.

PLEBISCITE TRIBUNALS

Beyond the isolation and neutralization of the local court system, the Plebiscite Commission must also consider the creation of new tribunals designed to serve the specific needs of the plebiscite process. Three types of tribunal are typically required:

1. A plebiscite tribunal to consider cases of political acts against the conduct of the plebiscite that would be inappropriate for the regular local courts.
2. A voter registration appeals board.
3. A vote contest board to hear accusations of fraud or of cheating in the casting and counting of the ballots.

1. Plebiscite Tribunal

A special tribunal is necessary to handle cases of a political character that bear upon the conduct of the plebiscite. Its jurisdiction would include offenses against the regulations and institutions of the Plebiscite Commission, falsification of documents relating to registration and voting, willful interference with the work of plebiscite officials, acts of impersonation during registration or voting, voting more than once, tampering with ballot papers, acts designed to prevent eligible citizens from voting, acts infringing the secrecy of the vote, threats of violence or of reprisal against voters or plebiscite officials. Penalties may include fines, suspension from office for public officials, imprisonment, and expulsion.

Typically, such a tribunal is composed of respected jurists from neutral countries. It may prove useful, as was the case in the Klagenfurt Basin plebiscite, to attach assessors representing the principal parties to the plebiscite, e.g., in Klagenfurt, an Austrian and a Yugoslav.[18] The assessors act only as consultants to the panel and do not take part in rulings or decisions. It is essential that the tribunal be served by a large staff that is provided sufficient resources to carry-out investigations and to process court documents quickly. Given the brief duration of most plebiscite regimes, justice delayed may mean no justice at all.

A plebiscite tribunal must be seen to be effective and efficient if it is to contribute to the establishment of the proper plebiscitary atmosphere. Interestingly, the simple presence of such a tribunal may be of such deterrent value that it may never be needed. In the Schleswig and Klagenfurt Basin plebiscites the tribunals were never put to work for lack of any cases.[19]

Finally, in order to deter post-election reprisals, the plebiscite tribunal should have a lifespan extending at least one year after the plebiscite vote. This will serve to underscore the seriousness of the penalties that the tribunal may impose.

2. Voter Registration Appeals Board

An accurate and complete electoral roll is a prerequisite for a troublefree election day. However, no matter now carefully and conscientiously the roll is prepared, there will be errors, omissions, and procedural grey areas. Thus, there must be a board to consider appeals from the rulings of the Registration Boards. The appeals board must have a sufficiently large staff to permit the investigation of original documents and the taking of depositions. Composed of experienced election officials or academics from outside countries, the appeals board must move rapidly and publicly--holding open hearings and providing written reasons for all of its decisions.

It is important to the success of the voter registration appeals process that the inhabitants of the plebiscite zone and potential outvoters be fully informed about complaint procedures. A public relations effort is needed to encourage residents to examine the electoral roll and to lodge complaints. It should be made clear where and how a complaint may be made. The local Registration Boards must inform dissatisfied complainants of their right to appeal and must make clear to them the procedure for doing so.

3. Vote Contest Board

The function of a vote contest board is to hear accusations of fraud or of cheating in the casting and counting of the ballots. If such accusations are found to be accurate, the board must then assess whether the damage was sufficient to materially alter the outcome of the vote. It should be noted that the function of this board is not the protection of the rights of individuals--that is a task for the court system.[20] The board's function is to ascertain whether the rules and procedures of the election have been violated or subverted. The board's members should be composed of experienced officials or academics drawn from outside the area who have spend several months in the plebiscite zone (1) familiarizing themselves with the political forces at play and (2) working with the Plebiscite Commission in the development of the final balloting and counting procedures.

The value of an independent vote contest board lies in its ability to cope authoritatively with the inevitable charges and countercharges that follow a plebiscite. Unlike the Plebiscite Commission, which has something of a vested interest in proclaiming the plebiscite a success, the vote contest board can credibly act to certify the overall validity--or invalidity--of the vote. Thus, it plays an essential role in demonstrating to the inhabitants of the plebiscite zone and to a skeptical world community that the "will of the people" has been accurately and honestly measured.

POLICE

If the courts are the working symbols of state power, the police are the cutting edge of that power. Hence, the immediate reorganization of the police has been vital to the success of plebiscites. Plebiscite administrators who have failed to reshape local police forces or who have been tardy in doing so have suffered severe losses in authority.

The first variable to be assessed in planning such a reorganization is the degree of politicization of the police force. Little reshaping is required if the antecedent state was free of statutes defining political crimes and if the police had earned a reputation for impartial treatment of minority and dissident groups. However, such an unpoliticized police force is most improbable in a plebiscite situation. Almost by definition, secessionist, irredentist, and national liberation struggles involve violence, sedition, arrests, and charges of treason. Thus, the local police inherited by a plebiscite regime from the antecedent state(s) are almost invariably politicized to some degree.

Extreme Politicization

In cases of extreme politicization, where the police have formed secret death squads to murder and to "disappear" (sic) dissidents, the only recourse for a plebiscite regime is to disband the police entirely and to expel them from the plebiscite area. The expulsion of the police will cause an uproar among the local people most closely tied to the old state. After years of secure protection by "their " policemen, they will understandably feel exposed and threatened. Nevertheless, there is no more dangerous category of people to have at large during a hotly contested plebiscite than sacked policemen.

The tasks of a disbanded police force can be taken over by a new, balanced force recruited from the local communities. However, in situations of high tension, one or more of the communities is likely to boycott the new police force--leaving it fatally imbalanced. Often there is simply insufficient time to hire and train a new force. Consequently, neutral troops must be used in lieu of civilian police. It should be noted that regular army troops require retraining if they are to perform police duties. Soldiers trained to respond in combat with maximum force must be reindoctrinated in the gentle arts of minimum force. Also, elite "shock" troops and soldiers hardened in combat make the worst policemen.

Moderate Politicization

In cases of moderate politicization of the local police, several strategies are open. One is to balance the ethnic or racial composition of the force by hiring new police officers from the minority community. In the Schleswig plebiscite this approach worked quite well with two Danish and two German officers being dispatched on every call.[21] The mixed patrol approach is the crux of the ethnic balance strategy. In Teschen, where intense ethnic animosities made mixed patrols impossible, Czech police patrolled the Czech-inhabited areas and Polish police patrolled in Polish areas. Thus, the Polish minority living in the Czech area and the Czechs in the Polish districts lived at the mercy of their enemies. This led in Teschen to a general breakdown of authority and was an important reason for the cancellation of the plebiscite.

If, because of time constraints or political obstacles, it proves impossible to balance the composition of the police force, an alternative strategy is to retain the existing force but to place them under intense neutral supervision. Inspectors may be recruited from neutral countries and should speak, if possible, the native languages of the plebiscite area. The inspectors should be assigned to every level of the police hierarchy and should, as much as possible, accompany the police on patrols and when answering calls. The presence of neutral officers can be enormously reassuring to those portions of the population who deeply distrust the regular police. The dispatch of 571 British policemen to serve as

Assistant Election Supervisors in the Zimbabwe-Rhodesia vote of 1980 is reported to have had a profound effect upon the voters.[22]

> The deployment of British policemen, unarmed and wearing their distinctive helmets as Assistant Supervisors, at most rural polling stations achieved a psychological breakthrough in reassuring the electorate of the secrecy of the ballot and the impartiality of polling staff. They played a valuable role, just by their presence, but most were active in useful ways helping voting to proceed smoothly. Above all their presence inside the polling stations had a calming influence. We would like to add our own tribute to the British authorities who conceived the idea, as well as to the policemen who saw it through so splendidly.[23]

New Appearance

An important part of the reorganization of the police under a plebiscite regime is a change in the appearance of the police. Uniforms should be altered or replaced. The Schleswig commission ordered the use of large badges displaying a shield trimmed with blue ribbon and emblazoned with the letters C.I.S. (Commission Internationale, Slesvig).[24] The Marienwerder Commission issued regulations "forbidding the members of the police force to maintain a military appearance" and ordered that all weapons (except dirks and pistols) be surrendered.[25] Thus, a "new look" police force must be established--a force neutral in its composition, impartial in its mission, and distinctive in its appearance.

NEUTRAL FORCES

The maintenance of public order is the prerogative of states. No state maintains public order in a wholly impartial manner. The laws and men of government favor some segments of society and discriminate against others. Through differential taxation, expenditure, regulation, and law enforcement, the public order reflects those groups that control the machinery of state. To those who are disaffected with a state and its brand of public order, the state presents a mailed fist--the police, the courts, the prisons, and, ultimately, the army. In a state torn by separatist and nationalist warfare, the security forces typically lose their professional detachment and become highly politicized. Thus, it is a first priority of a plebiscite regime to remove or neutralize the security forces of the antecedent state or states. The same applies to the armed forces the "shadow" states established by insurgent movements.

The conclusion of a ceasefire and the withdrawal of armies is a matter for negotiation that must be resolved by agreement before a plebiscite regime enters a territory to take-up its tasks. Past experience dictates that the troop withdrawal agreement should include a detailed schedule for withdrawal with clearly marked target dates. If necessary, a small monitoring group should be constituted to observe and to report compliance.

The vacuum created by the withdrawal of armies--especially of armies recently at war--must be filled by a contingent of neutral forces under the orders of the plebiscite regime. Since neither the United Nations nor any other international organization to this date maintains a standing force of its own neutral peacekeeping troops, neutral countries must be invited to contribute detachments to the force. The cost of deploying the neutral force has been paid in previous plebiscites from the normal tax revenues collected in the plebiscite area. If this is insufficient, states with an interest in a peaceful settlement may be invited to underwrite the remaining costs.

There are two differing approaches to the way in which neutral forces may be deployed in a plebiscite zone. In the words of an officer with the British contingent in the Saar (1935), there is the "Continental Method" and the "British Method."

> The first may be termed the "Continental Method," and consists in the main of placing machine guns, etc., at street corners. The second may be termed the "British Method." Its principles are:
>
> 1. To make an imposing parade of force BEFORE the trouble breaks out.
> 2. To keep the troops hidden away during the actual period of tension, leaving the maintenance of order, in the first instance, to the police.
> 3. To maintain a large mobile reserve.[26]

The so-called "British Method" has become the standard practice for neutral troops during plebiscites and internationally supervised elections. Thus, they must be provided with transport aircraft, helicopters, road transport, and a radio network running the length of the chain of command. Close liaison must be established between the different detachments, between the plebiscite regime and the various detachments, between the detachments and the local civil and police authorities, and between the detachments and the leaders of the parties participating in the plebiscite. It is also important that before issuing orders to the neutral forces, the plebiscite authorities should meet with the officers and non-coms to explain the reasons for the orders. If they are to behave with the tact and discretion necessary to accomplish their mission, the neutral forces must fully understand the political events going on about them.

The basic value of the neutral force is its reassuring presence--a guarantee of peace for the local inhabitants. Sound liaison between the forces and local community leaders is needed to smooth-out the occasional irritations that inevitably occur between soldiers and the neighboring civilian population. Creative public relations, such as the organizing of football matches between teams of plebiscite troops and local teams in the Saar (1935), can help to dissolve the image of the neutral forces as an army of occupation.[27]

Beyond the reassurance provided by their presence, the neutral forces may also be employed to patrol borders and remote areas in the plebiscite zone, to monitor compliance with ceasefire agreements, and to investigate serious incidents. Korbel provides a useful illustration of this role drawn from the experience of the United Nations observer forces in Kashmir.

> Illustrative not only of the necessity of the observers' work but also of its vexations is the case of the soldier seen bayoneting and burying a civilian. News of the incident spread rapidly. When it came to the ears of the UN observers, teams . . . set out for the spot. For seven days they struggled over exhausting terrain to reach the place of the incident. Upon their arrival they quickly established the facts. What the soldier had bayoneted and buried had been, not a civilian, but a wild dog!

> The case proved rather trivial, but it serves as a vivid illustration of the effectiveness of the day-to-day work of the United Nations observers. One can easily imagine that, had it not been for the prompt deflation of the word-of-mouth report, the rumor might have spread and grown: the lone civilian might easily have become a group of defenseless women and children and the simple soldier might have grown to a platoon.[28]

There is no general formula for the number of neutral forces needed to conduct a plebiscite. Indeed, it is possible, if the conditions are right, as in the Klagenfurt Basin, to conduct a plebiscite without the presence of neutral troops--if the political temperature is reasonably low, if the civilian population is largely unarmed, if the local security forces are reasonably professional and non-political. To the extent that these conditions do not apply, neutral troops will be needed. Since their function is to assist in the maintenance of calm--not to fight wars--the number of neutral troops is usually not more than a few thousand. The largest contingent, the nearly 200,000 employed in Upper Silesia, was needed to control two million bitterly divided Poles and Germans.

More typical in size was the 1300 man monitoring force in war-torn Zimbabwe-Rhodesia (1980)--a country the size of France. What distinguished the Zimbabwe-Rhodesia operation from others was that there was no withdrawal of troops. Both the Rhodesian army and the Black nationalist insurgents remained inside the country--contained for the most part in their bases and assembly areas. Thus, the role of the monitoring force was extremely delicate and, at times, quite risky. Brigadier Learmont, Deputy Commander of the monitoring force, tells of his doubts early in the operation.

> The consensus of opinion was that we were about to embark on a militarily disastrous enterprise, with the near certainty of being "taken out" the first night. . .[29]

Lord Soames, the then Governor of Southern Rhodesia, attributed the success of the monitoring operation to two factors:

> I believe it will be generally agreed that its success depended largely on two factors: on the fact that the neutral trooos were located WITH the opposing forces of either side, not BETWEEN them; and because the exercise was conducted within a predetermined time limit. There was, therefore, no question of the monitoring force patrolling boundary lines between the Security Forces and the Patriotic Front forces, with all the problems that that would have entailed. Neither was there any question of an open-ended commitment--although this circumstance did not make the operation any less risky from the point of view of the brave men who performed it.[30]

ASSEMBLY AREAS

A plebiscite cannot be conducted in the middle of a war. Clearly, an effective ceasefire is a prerequisite for the establishment of a plebiscitary atmosphere. Armies must retire to their bases and politicians must take-over the struggle. But what is done with armies that have no bases? Dozens of today's national liberation armies have no bases per se. In the imagery of Mao, they are fish swimming in a sea of civilian collaborators. What formal bases they do have are usually located in friendly neighboring countries.

Thus, there are two problems to be solved. First, how can voters in a plebiscite be safeguarded from intimidation by heavily armed, strongly motivated guerrilla fighters who live amongst portions of the civilian population? Second, how can the irregular fighters of such armies living secretly within the plebiscite zone and those living in camps located in neighboring countries participate in the balloting? The solution to these problems, as illustrated in the 1979-1980 Zimbabwe-Rhodesia vote, is the creation of Assembly Areas.

After a ceasefire takes effect, guerrilla soldiers (soldiers of non-state armies) report to predesignated locations where they are received by neutral officers of the Plebiscite Commission's observer force. Soldiers who report to the Assembly Areas are not disarmed and they remain under the command of their officers. (Indeed, men or women reporting to the Assembly Areas in Zimbabwe-Rhodesia without weapons were turned away by the monitoring force.) The soldiers then remain in the Assembly Area until (a) the plebiscite vote is held and (b) they cast their ballots at polling stations located in the Assembly Areas.

The key to the success of an Assembly Area operation is round-the-clock liaison between the monitoring force and the leaders of the insurgent armies. The monitoring force in Zimbabwe-Rhodesia, a multi-national group of some 1,300 men, supervised 14 Assembly Areas that ultimately housed 22,000 Patriotic Front fighters. Patriotic Front liaison personnel provided the "friction proofing" that made the operation work. They were instrumental in leading the first, deeply suspicious units into the Assembly Areas. Maintaining calm and resolving misunderstandings required considerable cooperation. Brigadier Learmont reported:

> Indeed there were several incidents of alarms caused by the sound of gun or mortar fire nearby which caused the Patriotic Front to react fairly dramatically. In the worst case they surrounded the complete Australian contingent at Assembly Place Echo with machine guns, RPG 7s and mortars trained on the Monitoring Force.[31]

Again, good liaison work defused the situation.

> After about a month of our presence the Patriotic Front had come to accept us totally, to place great trust in the way the Monitoring Force was handling things and had begun to cherish the hope that we would remain with them until such times as the Assembly Places closed down and all their inhabitants had reverted to normal life.[32]

The lessons learned by the Monitoring Force in Zimbabwe-Rhodesia should be studied closely by those who in the future seek to bring guerrilla wars and wars of national liberation to a peaceful conclusion.

BORDER TRAFFIC

A plebiscite zone must be isolated from the influence of neighboring states. When their interests are involved, states are easily tempted to meddle in the elections of other states. The temptation to interfere in a vote to determine sovereignty over an adjacent area can prove overwhelming. Non-governmental organizations within neighboring states--such as large business enterprises and ethnic organizations--may also seek to exert influence upon the outcome of a plebiscite. The first line of defense against all such influences is the border of the plebiscite zone. The actions of the Schleswig Commission were typical of most twentieth century plebiscite authorities. Wambaugh reports:

> An essential part of the Commission's plan of administration was the establishment of complete control over the entrance into and exit from the plebiscite area. It prepared an order to the effect that the borders of the area could be crossed only at certain specified points and that, to enter, all persons over eleven years of age must have passports, visaed for the plebiscite area both by the consul of the country of citizenship and by the passport officer of the Commission in Hamburg or Copenhagen, and endorsed also by the Danish or German authorities so that they might return to Germany or Denmark, respectively.[33]

In addition, the Schleswig Commission issued "border circulation cards" to residents living near the zone's border to enable them to cross back and forth as their regular routines required.

Strict control of border traffic is essential when tensions run high. There is a strong correlation between disorder during the run-up to a plebiscite vote and the inability of the plebiscite regime to control effectively the borders. The plebiscites in Upper Silesia and Sopron were disrupted and the planned plebiscites in Teschen and in Tacna-Arica were aborted to no small extent because of the actions of outside saboteurs, agents, organizers, and propagandists.[34]

As the day of the plebiscite vote approaches and as interest mounts, most plebiscite regimes place further restrictions upon entry to the plebiscite zone. The Commission in Upper Silesia limited entry to arriving outvoters, returning residents of the zone, and to non-residents who were granted special permission to enter.[35] On voting day itself, the Klagenfurt Basin Commission restricted entry to qualified voters only. The

Upper Silesia Commission, fearing bands of roving trouble-makers, banned the entry and exit of all motor vehicles.[36] The Saar Commission in 1935 established direct telephone lines linking Commission headquarters with the eleven main border posts in an effort to resolve quickly disputes over rights of entry.[37]

In situations where a plebiscite marks the end of a separatist or national liberation war, the plebiscite regime may also face a large influx of refugees and expelees seeking to return home. Often, these persons carry no documents and may have no home within the plebiscite zone to return to. Added to the problem of documenting and housing such persons is the risk that those coming from guerrilla bases and other sanctuary areas may attempt to bring weapons with them.

The control of border traffic requires a sizable commitment of manpower and logistical support. Nevertheless, it is essential to the integrity of the democratic process that only those legitimately entitled to participate in the plebiscite are allowed to do so.

DISTRICTS

An early task for the organizers of a plebiscite is the delimitation of the boundaries of the plebiscite area. Not infrequently,the contending parties will already be on record with claims to what they believe should be their sovereign territory. Often the claims are exaggerated in order to create bargaining chips for future negotiations. Agreement must be reached by the principal state and non-state parties to the dispute before the planning for a plebiscite may proceed.

Curiously, the prospect of a plebiscite tends to encourage the parties to reduce their more exaggerated claims to territory. This is so because an unreasonable boundary claim would include greater numbers of other nationalities or factions and thereby lessen the likelihood of electoral victory. A modest boundary including only areas densely inhabited by one's own people is the surest route to success. By the same token, a small area permits a greater concentration of one's organizational resources for the campaign. Thus, unlike nearly every form of inter-state negotiation--where exaggerated claims are the norm--the plebiscite encourages modest claims, claims that stand a chance of being upheld by the people in the territory at issue.

The next step is to determine the number and size of the electoral districts within the plebiscite zone. It may be decided that the entire zone should be treated en bloc. This may be done in situations such as the Saar where the area is ethnically, geographically, and economically homogeneous. More commonly, plebiscites are held in response to situations of heterogeneity with different regions pulling in different directions. To measure such heterogeneity, a pattern of voting districts must be laid down with a sufficiently fine mesh to catch and record the diversity. However, districts that are too small tend to undermine the secrecy of the ballot and thereby invite reprisals. It was suggested in Schleswig (1920) that rural districts with only four or five voters should be merged together into larger districts.[38] Otherwise, the parties to the plebiscite could easily pinpoint how specific families or small hamlets had voted.

The specific demarcation of districts is best done by a commission composed of members from neutral countries. They should be advised by a balanced panel of local residents. The drawing-up of electoral districts is a thankless task in the best of circumstances and the end-product seldom satisfies all parties equally.

TURNOUT

A high turnout is vital to the credibility of a plebiscite. This is so because both the inhabitants of a plebiscite zone and international opinion must be satisfied that the views of the entire plebiscite population have indeed been expressed. A low poll can be seen as a protest against the manner in which a plebiscite has been conducted. It can be read as the product of intimidation or of misinformation on the part of the inhabitants. The 1979 devolution referendum in Scotland was approved by a narrow majority of those who voted but was fatally undermined by a markedly low turnout.

A plebiscite regime can encourage a high turnout in several ways. Adequate time and resources must be spent preparing a complete electoral roll. A publicity campaign explaining to the electorate the precise manner in which ballots are cast is also important. In Zimbabwe-Rhodesia, a film entitled "How to Vote" was produced and shown in cinemas throughout the country.[39] It is important that there be a large number of clearly marked and conveniently located polling stations. (Of course, the larger the number of polling stations, the larger the problem of ballot security.) Mobile polling stations that can make a circuit of remote villages, as was done in Zimbabwe-Rhodesia, can also prove useful.[40]

It is usually a mistake to leave the bulk of the "get out the vote" effort to the parties contesting the plebiscite. This is so because often one of the parties (e.g., the Austrians in the Klagenfurt Basin) will possess vastly superior organizational and manpower resources compared to the other parties. Such an imbalance will be viewed as unfair by the less organized communities. This, in turn, may produce calls for the plebiscite vote to be delayed until the less organized can become better organized--an idea that will be bitterly opposed by the well organized community. Worse still, the leaders of the underorganized communities may call upon their people to boycott the vote in protest.

Most of the successful plebiscites of the twentieth century have produced a turnout in excess of 90 percent. Citizens who are cynical of the Tweedledum and Tweedledee politicians and parties that contest domestic elections become actively concerned when the choice is between Polish or German citizenship, a White minority regime or a Black majority regime. Plebiscites fail where large segments of the population boycott the plebiscite and where potential voters have been frightened away from the polls by warnings of reprisal.

PLEBISCITARY ATMOSPHERE

A plebiscitary atmosphere can be defined as a state of readiness by an electorate to address openly the issue of sovereignty. It is a close cousin to the more familiar electoral atmosphere that precedes competitive elections in liberal democracies, i.e., a readiness by a people and government to play by the rules and to abide by the result. It is an atmosphere that encourages reflection, discussion, and open campaigning conducted without fear of intimidation or reprisal. Such a pre-election atmosphere is taken for granted in stable democracies. Yet it is this atmosphere as much as the actual vote itself that makes an election valid. If an election is conceived in an atmosphere of violence and coercion, it will not be viewed as valid. Those on the losing side will repudiate it. Even the victors may regret that their mandate to rule has been compromised. It is not surprising that such elections are often annulled by revolution or coup d'etat.

In a plebiscite, the pre-vote atmosphere is critical. The failure to establish a plebiscitary atmosphere has been the reason for the abandonment of several plebiscites. The plebiscite commission in Tacna and Arica struggled for ten months to create the conditions for a free and open vote. General John Pershing was the President of the Commission. Wambaugh reports:

> He felt that a free and fair plebiscite meant that the voters of both sides should have equal opportunities and that the obligations to provide such conditions rested squarely on the shoulders of the government in charge of the civil administration of the territory. Finding that the informal representations regarding conditions had no effect, he now felt that the situation had shown itself to be such that the Commission must demand the taking of positive steps to establish the sort of freedom essential to the holding of a fair plebiscite. When the Commission met again, on October 8, 1925, General Pershing announced that he was convinced that the free and fair plebiscite contemplated in the Award could not be held until the Government of Chile should put an end to the oppression being practised on part of the inhabitants by the officials and societies which counted on toleration by it; and that it should openly repudiate the existing situation by demonstrating in the area that the regime of repression by means of soldiers, carabineros, police, secret police,and partisan officials, had been replaced by a regime respectful of the rights of both parties, which would not permit, now or later, the calling to account of anyone for his sentiments or his vote.[41]

The Chilean view was uncompromising:

> Chile cannot with equanimity stand and see the advantages of a war which she did not provoke, the bloodshed of the pick and flower of her manhood in those days, forty-two years of sacrifice and effort to make these territories what they are; the sacrifice of the favorable position which she held under the Treaty of

> Ancon, and which the Award recognized as perfectly legitimate; she cannot see all this forgotten and thrown to the winds in the name of the vague, incomprehensible and purposeless phrase of "atmosphere" and futile accusations of intimidation. . .[42]

Ultimately, the plebiscite was abandoned.

On first glance, the prospects for the establishment of a plebiscitary atmosphere in areas rocked by civil war seem remote. Yet there are cases of such an atmosphere being created in the most remarkable circumstances. Upper Silesia is a sound early illustration but the recent success of internationally supervised elections in war-torn Zimbabwe-Rhodesia and ravaged Uganda is an even more dramatic demonstration.

A plebiscitary atmosphere is largely a matter of balance. In the words of Lord Soames, the British Governor who supervised the Zimbabwe-Rhodesia vote, the key dynamic is "a balance of trust--or, if you prefer, of mistrust."[43] Rather than viewing himself as the inventor of a pre-election "humanitarian utopia," he saw his role as that of referee:

> As the referee, I wanted to see the game played to a finish. But I could not simply turn a blind eye to malpractices going on in some of the scrimmages. Nor on the other hand did I want, if I could avoid it, to award so many penalty kicks to one side that the other walked off the pitch--as well it might. In short, the only way to see the game through to the end was to blow the whistle from time to time so that a measure of rough justice could be done--and be seen to be done.[44]

Once the balance is struck between the sides, it develops a self-reinforcing robustness. Acts of intimidation or of disruption are viewed by all parties as a threat to the validity of the result--to the legitimacy of subsequent regimes. The plebiscite is often seen as the one best chance for a strife-weary population to secure a peaceful future.

TIMING AND MOMENTUM

In most circumstances the entire duration of a plebiscite--from the opening of the Plebiscite Conference to the establishment of the new sovereignty arrangement--should not take more than five to seven months. Of course, it may take years--even decades--for the conditions appropriate for a plebiscite to emerge. Once those conditions do emerge and a Plebiscite Conference is convened, the momentum toward the final conduct of the plebiscite vote must be sustained. Thus, the Plebiscite Conference should go into almost continuous session until agreement is reached and a Plebiscite Commission is constituted and dispatched to the plebiscite zone. The Plebiscite Commission should be given a free hand to prepare the zone for the vote. As indicated in the Time Frame chart, the preliminary tasks of the Commission should not take over two to three months. Once a proper plebiscitary atmosphere has been established in the zone, a three to four week official campaign period can commence. The date of the vote should be left to the discretion of the Commission. The vote, held on a Sunday or special holiday to encourage a large turnout, is then followed by a one to two week period for counting and verifying the vote. The Commission then reports the results, along with its recommendations concerning sovereignty, to the Plebiscite Conference. The Conference resumes its session, makes its final decisions concerning new sovereignty arrangements for the zone, and, together with the Commission, works-out the details of the transitional period. Following a transitional period of not less than a month, the Plebiscite Commission relinquishes authority over the zone and departs. The Plebiscite Conference adjourns _sine die_.

PLEBISCITE TIME FRAME

PHASE	DURATION
Plebiscite Conference	One to two months.
Plebiscite Commission Preliminary Tasks: neutralization of administration, troop withdrawal and pacification, return of outvoters, compile and verify electoral roll, ballot mechanics	Two to three months.

Campaign	Three to four weeks.
Vote	One or two days.
Counting and Certification of Vote	One to two weeks.
Plebiscite Conference Resumes and Transitional Period to New Sovereignty Arrangement	One to three months.

Thus, five to seven months should, given the lessons of earlier plebiscites, be sufficient to carry-out a plebiscite. The British-administered election in Zimbabwe-Rhodesia took just six months from the start of the Lancaster House Conference to the end of the transition period installing the new government in power.[45] Only seventy days elapsed between the arrival of the new British Governor, Lord Soames, and the successful conclusion of the election. It was an achievement that was not thought possible at the time by most informed observers of southern African affairs. The key to the success of the Zimbabwe-Rhodesia operation was the maintenance of momentum. Bold strokes were taken to cut through obstacles. Short cuts were performed on occasion as well.[46]

Some plebiscites do not "go by the book" and may require a longer preparatory or transitional period. Thus, the Plebiscite Conference should grant the Plebiscite Commission a period of up to two years to conduct the plebiscite. The power to determine the timing of the various phases of the plebiscite is an important tool in the hands of the Commission. It makes it more difficult for the parties to the plebiscite to either stampede or stonewall the Commission into holding the vote at an inopportune time. Additional months may be required to assist parties that were proscribed by the antecedent state(s) to organize sufficiently to become meaningful participants in the plebiscite. Neutralization of the civil administration and the police may prove exceedingly difficult. The withdrawal of troops and the deployment of neutral observer forces may encounter unanticipated delays. Thus the Plebiscite Commission needs the ability to adjust the plebiscite timetable to meet unexpected developments.

Circumstances may arise where an extended period of neutral, international administration may be desirable in an area before the conduct of a plebiscite vote. In such cases the fifteen year tenure of the Saar Governing Commission could prove a valuable model. The experience and expertise of the United Nations Trusteeship Council could also be invaluable in establishing an interim, neutral administration. Indeed, one option that should be considered for future plebiscites is an option for a period of neutral administration leading to a second plebiscite at a later date.

NOTES

[1]Johannes Mattern, The Employment of the Plebiscite in the Determination of Sovereignty (Baltimore: The Johns Hopkins Press, 1920), p. 85.

[2]Stein Rokkan, Citizens, Elections, Parties (Oslo: Universitetsforlaget, 1970), p. 166.

[3]Colin Baker, "Conducting the Elections in Zimbabwe 1980," Public Administration and Development, Vol. 2, No. 1, January-March 1983, p. 58.

[4]Sarah Wambaugh, The Saar Plebiscite (Cambridge: Harvard University Press, 1940), p. 90.

[5]The aborted attempt at a plebiscite in Tacna and Arica was a clear illustration of the need for complete administrative control over the plebiscite zone. The Chilean administration thwarted every attempt of the Plebiscite Commission to create fair and impartial conditions for the vote.

[6]Josef Korbel, Danger in Kashmir (Princeton: Princeton University Press, Revised Edition, 1966), pp. 118-164.

[7]Sarah Wambaugh, Plebiscites Since the World War (Washington, DC: Carnegie Endowment for International Peace, 1933), p. 496.

[8]Korbel, pp. 132-133.

[9]Southern Rhodesia Elections: February 1980. The Report of the Commonwealth Observer Group on elections leading to independent Zimbabwe (London: Commonwealth Secretariat, 1980), p. 22.

[10]Southern Rhodesia Elections, p. 56.

[11]Wambaugh, Plebiscites, p. 117.

[12]Wambaugh, Saar, p. 288.

[13]Wambaugh, Plebiscites, p. 498.

[14]Wambaugh, Plebiscites, p. 116. For the 1975 plebiscite in the Mariana Islands District of the Trust Territory of the Pacific Islands the following procedure was adopted: "The Secretarial Order provided that the

Chief Justice of the High Court of the Trust Territory should appoint one or more justices of that Court as a Special Plebiscite Appellate Court with exclusive jurisdiction over all appeals from rulings of the Plebiscite Voter Registration Board. Appeals were to be heard before a single judge of the Special Plebiscite Appellate Court. Rulings of the Court were to be final." Report of the United Nations Visiting Mission to Observe the Plebiscite in the Mariana Islands District, Trust Territory of the Pacific Islands, June 1975, T/1771, p. 27.

[15]It should be noted that even in the best of times public servants are "a blend of the good and the not-so-good." Southern Rhodesia Elections, p. 21.

[16]Wambaugh, Plebiscites, pp. 225-226.

[17]Southern Rhodesia Elections, p. 12.

[18]Wambaugh, Plebiscites, p. 465.

[19]Wambaugh, Plebiscites, p. 466.

[20]Geoffrey Hand, Jacques Georgel, and Christoph Sasse (eds.) European Electoral Systems Handbook (London: Butterworths, 1979), p. 81.

[21]Wambaugh, Plebiscites, p. 95.

[22]Southern Rhodesia Elections, p. 66.

[23]Southern Rhodesia Elections, pp. 66-67.

[24]Wambaugh, Plebiscites, p. 68.

[25]Wambaugh, Plebiscites, p. 117.

[26]Wambaugh, Saar, p. 285.

[27]Wambaugh, Saar, p. 286.

[28]Korbel, pp. 162-163.

[29]J.H. Learmont, "Reflections from Rhodesia," Royal United Services Institute Journal, December 1980, p. 49.

[30]Lord Soames, "From Rhodesia to Zimbabwe," International Affairs, Vol. 56, No. 3, Summer 1980, p. 413.

[31]Learmont, pp. 53-54.

[32]Learmont, p. 53.

[33]Wambaugh, Plebiscites, p. 71.

[34]Wambaugh, Plebiscites, p. 499.

[35]Wambaugh, Plebiscites, p. 467.

[36]Wambaugh, Plebiscites, p. 467.

[37]Wambaugh, Saar, p. 298.

[38]Wambaugh, Plebiscites, p. 89.

[39]Southern Rhodesia Elections, pp. 293-297. "In the 1956 Togoland plebiscite, conducted under the auspices of the United Nations Trusteeship Council, the Information Services Department undertook an intensive campaign to give publicity to the alternatives at issue and to educate

the people on the qualifications and the procedure for registering as a voter. Sixteen mobile cinema vans set out on 3 January on itineraries drawn up in consultation with the district authorities. One hundred and fifty thousand copies of a pamphlet entitled 'How to Register' in English, Twi, Ewe, Dagbani and Hausa were distributed." Report of the Plebiscite Administrator on the plebiscite held in Togoland under British administration on 9 May 1956. T/1269, p. 2.

[40]Baker, p. 48.

[41]Wambaugh, Plebiscites, pp. 363-364.

[42]Wambaugh, Plebiscites, pp. 377-378.

[43]Soames, p. 412.

[44]Soames, p. 413.

[45]Baker, p. 46.

[46]Soames, pp. 411-412.

4

The Plebiscite Vote

IDENTIFICATION

The Plebiscite Commission must take steps to insure that only *bona fide* inhabitants of the plebiscite zone participate in the plebiscite process. Thus, the issuance of new identity cards--containing either photographs or thumbprints--is often necessary. Such documents are essential if the Plebiscite Commission is to monitor entry and exit into the plebiscite zone, to exclude outsiders from political meetings, and to insure reliable identification of qualified voters at the polling stations. In Upper Silesia identity cards were required for all inhabitants over age fifteen and were to be produced upon demand by any official.[1] Those who could not prove *bona fide* residence in the zone (and were thus refused identity cards) were required to depart from the zone within fifteen days.

If, during the plebiscite campaign, meetings and rallies are disrupted by intruders, it may be necessary for the Plebiscite Commission to order that all political meetings be "closed," that is, entry will be by card only. The Plebiscite Commission, together with the recognized parties to the plebiscite, may therefore print membership cards that must be shown to police officers before entering all closed meetings. Thus, zealots will be limited in their ability to disrupt meetings of other parties.

Accurate identification is of such importance to the conduct of the plebiscite--and to the ability of the inhabitants to participate in the plebiscite--that significant manpower and resources must be invested in it.

VOTER QUALIFICATION AND REGISTRATION

If a plebiscite is a mechanism for measuring the "will of the people," it is necessary that "the people" be defined precisely. The matter of who is qualified to vote is of such central importance that it must be outlined by the state and non-state parties at the Plebiscite Conference--leaving only the details to the Plebiscite Commission. The Saar plebiscite (1935) provides an illustration of what is required to demonstrate who is qualified and who is not qualified to vote. Wambaugh recounts to us the principles used in the Saar:

> . . . all persons, without distinction of sex or nationality, should have the right to vote who had completed their twentieth year at the date of the voting and possessed the status of resident in the Territory on June 28, 1919, and provided that this status of "resident" should be attributed to anyone who had had his or her habitual residence in the Territory on the date mentioned and had settled there with the intention of remaining. If the intention was not expressed, it might be deduced from records and documents in public offices, or from other kinds of evidence. If habitual residence were proved, the intent to remain must be presumed in the absence of reasons to suppose the contrary. Neither temporary presence on the date stipulated in the Treaty, nor temporary absence on that date, as for example, for military service, for study, or because of imprisonment or expulsion, would affect the status of the resident, nor would the mere fact of having performed military service in the Territory confer the status, nor residence there on military or civilian service purely in connection with the military occupation. The residence of minors and of persons under legal disability on the date stipulated must be considered to be that of the parent or guardian, except for a minor living apart and earning his own living. The residence of a married woman would be that of the husband, unless the two were legally separated or the wife had established her own separate habitual residence. Those under legal disability were

> excluded from the vote, as were those committed to an asylum for the insane and those who, res adjudicata, had lost their civil rights, unless it were for a political offense.[2]

Often, the most politically sensitive element of the voter qualification standard is the specific date of habitual residence in the zone. The choice of date determines which immigrants, emigrants, and refugees will be included or excluded from voting. The differing habitual residence dates for several of the plebiscites held in 1920 reflect the politics of inclusion and exclusion in each zone:

ZONE	HABITUAL RESIDENCE DATE
Schleswig	January 1, 1900
Allenstein	January 5, 1905
Marienwerder	January 1, 1914
Upper Silesia	January 1, 1904
Klagenfurt Basin	January 1, 1912

To see the importance of the habitual residence date, imagine a plebiscite held today in the Israeli-occupied West Bank in which the habitual residence date was set at January 1, 1947. Compare this to a date of July 1, 1967 or January 1, 1983. The composition of the electorate would change significantly depending upon which date was selected.

Registration

Registration constitutes the acid test for voter qualification. It is the point where it is learned if the rules are indeed exhaustive and mutually exclusive.

There are two approaches to the task of voter registration. One is registration by application and the other registration by compilation. In registration by application, each potential voter must take the initiative to apply for inclusion on the electoral register. There are several advantages to registration by application. A full set of data can be acquired from each applicant--names, dates, places, occupations, children, parents--that is useful in determining eligibility to vote and, if needed, in crossing-checking applications later. The disadvantages of this system are, however, of a serious nature. It rewards those parties to the plebiscite that are well organized early in the plebiscite process and penalizes those who are unorganized or who are slow to organize. The Poles of Upper Silesia, for instance, were poorly organized compared to the Germans--since for years the German government had prohibited Polish political organizations on pain of imprisonment. The application system also gives those wishing to intimidate voters a second opportunity to keep them from voting--the other being on voting day.

The other approach is registration by compilation wherein registration boards compile lists of eligible voters from available records. Hence, qualified voters are automatically registered. (Those whose names do not emerge from the compilation process may apply for registration using a standard form.) The advantages of the compilation system are clear. It is less dependent upon organizations to stimulate registrations and there is less danger of intimidation. The disadvantages are a greater likelihood of error (duplicate registrations, names confused, misspellings) and of fraud by the employees who compile the lists.

At least a month should be allotted to the drawing-up of the electoral roll with either system. Once completed, it must be published and made readily available for public inspection. Residents should be encouraged to file claims for entry to the list, removal from the list, or corrections to the list. In the Saar (1935) the breakdown of claims and of claims ultimately allowed by the registration boards were:[3]

CLAIMS	TOTAL NUMBER	CLAIMS ALLOWED	PER CENT
For additional names	32,854	18,540	56.4
For removal of names	46,033	7,217	15.6
For corrections	28,258	28,210	99.08

Nearly all the errors were innocent ones deriving from illegible and incomplete records or from simple clerical errors. Some names caused confusion because of variant spellings, e.g., the name Gerstener could be spelt Gerstner, Garstner, Garstener, Karstener, Karstner, Kerstner, or Kerstener.[4]

A correction period of up to thirty days to allow full public scrutiny is necessary. Then, several weeks must be allowed for claims to be evaluated by the registration boards. Finally, time must be provided for appeals to the Registration Appeals Board. At every step of the claims and appeals process, written reasons must be provided for all rulings.

In the interest of building maximum confidence in the accuracy of the electoral roll, it is useful to permit parties to the plebiscite to submit claims as well as individuals. Outside observers and journalists should be encouraged to examine and spot check for errors in the roll and to witness the appeals process. Complete public confidence in the accuracy of the roll is an important step toward achieving public confidence in the validity of the plebiscite as a whole.

Election Without Registration

In normal circumstances registration is a necessary prerequisite for a free, accurate poll. However, there are circumstances when the compilation of a voter register is all but impossible. This was the case in wartorn Zimbabwe-Rhodesia in 1980. Colin Baker, an election supervisor on the Election Commission staff, explains:

> The absence of a register of voters was inevitable. First, there was insufficient time in which to prepare one: maintaining the momentum was a vital part of Britain's approach to the Lancaster House conference and to implementing the agreement in order to minimize political uncertainty and the risk of a breakdown in the cease-fire. Secondly, Zimbabwe had been at war for seven years and war-like conditions continued even after the agreement had been signed: guerrillas, even when gathered in Assembly Points, were not disarmed, acts of terrorism continued, old land mines remained buried on the roads. Thirdly, there were still many thousands of people absent from their homes as refugees both inside and outside the country, and the guerrillas themselves had good reason for not revealing their identities by registering. More than half a million people had left their homes and were living in Protected Villages; a further three quarters of a million had moved to the relative safety of peri-urban areas; and another quarter of a million were refugees in neighboring countries. In Goromonzi District the District Commissioner

> estimated that the number of adults in his District had fallen from 300,000 to 80,000 during the previous nine months. In such circumstances, the preparation of a register of voters was out of the question. Fourthly, the war had so depleted the country's available administrative manpower strength that it is very unlikely that sufficient personnel could have been made available to compile a register.[5]

How, then, were eligible voters identified at the polls and kept from voting several times at different polling stations? Polling officials estimated the age of those appearing at the polling stations and, when in doubt, demanded documents to prove age. Habitual residence was also guestimated by the polling officials. Seldom was proof demanded. It was their view, given the circumstances, that "few in their right senses would be in Zimbabwe unless they were citizens or permanently resident in the country!"[6] Multiple voting was impeded by requiring every voter to dip his fingers into a colorless dye (that remained on the fingers for several days) and that showed-up under ultraviolet light. Every prospective voter was required to place his hands into an ultraviolet "black box" to see if he had voted previously.

Thus, a successful internationally supervised election was conducted without a system of voter registration. Undoubtedly, some ineligible persons did vote and there were loud charges of multiple voting, e.g., that "Coca Cola, Russian toothpaste, or sheep's urine" could wash-off the dye.[7] If the vote had not been so unexpectedly lopsided, these perceived flaws could have tainted the result. Nevertheless, it does demonstrate that a successful vote can be conducted in circumstances that do not permit voter registration.

OUTVOTERS

Sovereignty struggles seem invariably to produce a mixed assortment of castaways: exiles, refugees, emigres, expellees, and a host of simple emigrants seeking a more settled life elsewhere. The Belfast family that moves to Australia, the Somali living in a refugee camp in Kenya, the P.L.O. sympathizer deported from the West Bank, all are native born sons and daughters of their respective nations who, given the vicissitudes of history, find themselves in exile. If there are plebiscites in the future pertaining to their respective homelands, which should be permitted to return and vote?

Persons living outside a plebiscite zone but who are designated as qualified voters are called outvoters. Areas that have suffered extended periods of violence and disorder often produce large numbers of outvoters--sometimes spread across the globe. The definition of an outvoter is a highly political matter. Since it bears on the question of who "the people" are in a plebiscite zone, it must be decided at the highest level, meaning, at the Plebiscite Conference. All decisions that define outvoters have an unequal impact upon the potential voting strength of the parties to a plebiscite. In Schleswig, the German party gained ground against the Danish party for two reasons. The Germans had the manpower and the resources to trackdown pro-German outvoters, to assist them to register, and even to pay for their transportation back to Schleswig to vote. Confronted with a total of four plebiscites that year (1920), the Germans created a central organization to trace, register, and transport German outvoters to all four plebiscites.[8] Trains were chartered, lodgings booked, even concert and theatre tickets provided to attract German outvoters. The Danish outvoter effort was amateur by comparison. The other advantage held by the Germans was the fact that most German outvoters resided in Germany while many Danish outvoters had emigrated to America. There was little hope of bringing significant numbers of these back to Schleswig. Permitting outvoters to cast absentee ballots from their current countries of residence would ease much of the burden for such people but would open the floodgates of fraud and intimidation. Picture the difference between Polish outvoters casting absentee ballots from Chicago (U.S.A.) and from Lvov (U.S.S.R.).

The outvoter issue is complex. Should the children of state officials briefly posted in the zone and who were born in the zone be designated as outvoters? Should the children of long-term refugees born outside the zone be eligible to vote in a land they may never have seen? Should an emigrant, now a settled citizen of another country, be classified an outvoter? A further complication is added by the common practice of stripping citizenship from persons who vote in foreign elections. Would a Lebanese citizen of Canada jeopardize that citizenship by voting in a plebiscite in Lebanon?

Once the outvoters for a plebiscite have been

defined, the Plebiscite Commission must move quickly to register them and to insure their unhindered travel to the plebiscite zone. Often, accommodation must be provided for refugees and deportees who have no home or family in the zone. Occasionally, a limited immunity from prosecution is offered to returning outvoters for alleged offenses committed prior to the plebiscite period. Any arrests of outvoters must be carefully reviewed to guard against politically-motivated police intimidation. The arrival of outvoters--typically treated as returning heros by their friends and viewed as enemy aliens by their opponents--raises the political temperature of a plebiscite. Without adequate protection, outvoters can suffer the fate of a group of Peruvian outvoters arriving in Tacna (1926). At the train station they were set upon by a large Chilean crowd that "attacked them with fists, kicks and sticks. . . There followed, at the exit from the station, and in the public streets of Tacna, a prolonged brutal and public mobbing of the Peruvians, who were endeavoring to proceed, partly in autos and partly on foot, toward the center of the city. . . Many Peruvians were injured, some seriously."[9]

The outvoter brings a dimension to the plebiscite that is lacking in most domestic elections. Given the record number of refugees and exiles overlaying the contemporary global landscape, it is almost certain that outvoters will feature prominently in future plebiscites.

CAMPAIGNING

Some may ask, "Why have a campaign at all? Won't Poles vote for joining Poland? Basques for a Basque state? White South Africans for a White South Africa? In matters of identity, can a campaign really change anyone's mind?" The answer is, yes, campaigns are important in plebiscites because (1) perceptions of identity are often complex and contradictory and (2) variables such as economic interest and state loyalty can outweigh national identity in determining how one votes.

(1) National Identity

The identity of an individual living in a long established, compact nation-state is a tidy affair. Identity is not an issue for the Parisian who views himself as French, is loyal to the French state, and who views the health of the French economy as co-terminus with his own economic health. Such tidiness is the exception. Is the villager in the Atlas Mountains a Berber? a Moroccan? a member of the Arab world? of the Islamic world? Is the German-speaking farmer living near Bolzano an Italian? a Tyrolian? an Austrian? a German? a European? (He is an Italian citizen. He considers himself Tyrolian and wants to join Austria. He views himself as part of the German nation and is a staunch European because the European Community's Common Agricultural Policy is making him rich.)

There is no clear correlation between national identity and the way one votes in a plebiscite. This is so chiefly because one's national identity may be unclear. The Polish government assumed that the Polish-speaking people of Allenstein and Marienwerder (1920) would vote to join Poland. However, some of these Polish-speakers considered themselves Mazurians--not Poles. Many others were Protestants and greatly preferred union with a Protestant Prussia rather than with a Catholic Poland. Other Polish-speakers, who considered themselves Poles and who were Catholic, still voted against joining Poland. They were repelled by the sight of Russian Bolshevik armies advancing through Polish territory in the days just prior to the plebiscite.

A plebiscite in the Klagenfurt Basin (1920) was thought superfluous by many. Obviously, it was argued, the Slovene population of the Basin will want to join their fellow Slovenes in Yugoslavia. Not so. The Basin's Slovene population faced an awkward choice. Either they would remain a minority group in a German dominated Austria or they could unite with the Slovenes of Yugoslavia and be a minority group in a Serbian and Croatian dominated Yugoslavia. Most chose minority status in Austria.

(2) Other Variables

Voting is influenced by perceptions of economic interest. A Basque may dream of an independent homeland but vote for the party that can cut the best deal for him in Madrid. Much of North America is populated by the descendants of people who--for a variety of reasons--forsook their homelands to acquire a new identity. Religious, ideological, regional, and state loyalties are important determinants of the way people vote in free, competitive elections. The many inaccurate predictions that have been made of the outcomes of plebiscites (and of internationally supervised elections) are testimony to this behavioral fact of political life.

Campaign Organization. An open, vigorously contested election campaign serves to reassure both the voters and the world community of the fairness and legitimacy of the vote. It is the responsibility of the Plebiscite Commission to lay down the ground rules of the campaign. It must establish a framework within which the parties to the plebiscite can actively organize their supporters, engage in publicity and propaganda activities, and gain fair access to the mass media.

The first step is the licensing of the official parties to the plebiscite. The Commission may choose to certify only as many party organizations as there are options in the plebiscite ballot. In the Saar (1935), for instance, there were three options: union with Germany, union with France, and maintenance of the *status quo* (the international regime). Hence, three party organizations were licensed by the Commission. Alternatively, a Commission could permit as many official campaign organizations as there are major viewpoints on the ballot options. The important thing is that no indigenous group or viewpoint feels excluded from the campaign.

Membership in a party organization is normally restricted to qualified voters in the plebiscite zone. Civil servants and policemen are usually prohibited from membership or any form of participation in the campaign. Rules must be established governing the election of party leaders, the raising and disbursement of party funds, and other routine organizational matters. Most plebiscite commissions have required that the parties provide at least two days advance notice of all meetings and rallies. In the Saar (1935) the commission ordered that halls be requisitioned if a party could show that it was being denied reasonable access to meeting facilities.[10]

A campaign is an exercise in communication. Its basic aim is to provide information that will reawaken and reinforce existing predispositions held by the voter. Rarely does a campaign convert. It builds upon what is already there--pride in one's culture, hopes for a better future, mistrust of foreigners, trust in particular leaders, concern for one's retirement, worry at the prospect of unemployment, a sense of affiliation to a political party, a fear of war. A campaign activates such predispositions (1) through the distribution of printed information, (2) through the staging of campaign events,

(3) through canvassing and personal contact, and (4) through the mass media. Each of these modes of campaign communication must be supervised by the Plebiscite Commission to assure fair and reasonably balanced access to them.

Campaign Themes. The main campaign themes developed in a plebiscite campaign denote the sort of predispositions the parties wish to reawaken in the voter. The message on a poster published by the Danish party in the Schleswig plebiscite (1920) developed several themes:

> Why should you vote for Denmark? I. Because your race is Danish; II. Because Flensburg will die if cut off from North Schleswig; III. Because no other country takes better care of its children and aged; IV. Because in Denmark a man earns as many kroner as he does marks in Germany; V. Because the Danish krone buys eight times as much as the German mark.[11]

An Austrian post in the Klagenfurt Basin (1920), picturing a destitute family, declared:

> The Yugoslav State is not awake to its duty to care for the worker![12]

A 1980 Zimbabwe-Rhodesia poster entitled "Marxism Socialism"--undoubtedly published by White Rhodesians but aimed at the Black population--pictured a tough-looking Black revolutionary cadre standing in front of a class of young Black students. The poster declared:

> Those who are supported by Communist Russia claim they will give everyone free education. But the truth is that they will destroy your children. Under their rule, there is total control over what your children will be taught at school. They will be forced to learn Marxist-Socialist politics.
>
> There will be total control over the choice of job for every child.
>
> They must work where the State decides. They cannot work for themselves.
>
> They cannot choose their own job.

> They cannot choose a career which suits their abilities and interests, and they cannot study to be experts in jobs of their own choice.
>
> This form of Socialism is a trick! This form of Socialism will destroy your children.[13]

Most of the plebiscite commissions have permitted such propaganda as the above requiring only that (1) advance copies be provided to the commission's legal department for screening, (2) that the name of the licensed party organization appear on it, and (3) that the name of the printer or, in the case of tapes, the producer (who must be a local resident and qualified voter) also appears.

Goods Propaganda. The Schleswig plebiscite (1920) saw the development of a forthright technique designed to appeal to the economic sensitivities of the voter. The inhabitants of Schleswig,like those of the rest of Germany, had been subsisting on a grim diet of

> bread, potatoes, and salt, who had no butter and scarcely any milk, and whose schools were closed for lack of coal. The daily sight of automobiles coming from Denmark laden with butter, pork, tea, and coffee to be distributed free was as pointed as it was silent. Danish committees also invited the German trade unions to send ailing children to Denmark for a week's outing, and it is said that as many as ten thousand children were entertained in this way. The Danes insist that this was all for charity, with no political purpose whatever, but the Germans say that the automobiles with food came no more after the vote was counted.[14]

Such "goods propaganda" was also in evidence in the Klagenfurt Basin plebiscite (1920). In other cases, the supply of vital goods was blocked by neighboring states to intimidate the plebiscite voters. Thus, a Plebiscite Commission must make arrangement with neighboring states to ensure that normal supplies arrive smoothly and that consumer goods are not brazenly flaunted for the purpose of influencing the plebiscite vote. Of course, if the option in the plebiscite is between the zone joining a prosperous state or a destitute state, it would be unrealistic to insist that the campaign ignore economic reality.

Access to the Mass Media. Provision must be made for balanced access by the official parties to the press, radio, and television. Since in most of the world radio and television are directly controlled by the state, the Plebiscite Commission will inherit control over such facilities in the plebiscite zone. Thus, a simple formula that balances air time can be devised. Perhaps the best way to achieve balance in the print media is to encourage the proliferation of independent and party-owned newspapers. Such was the case during the internationally supervised election in Uganda (1980):

> Every political party had two or more papers providing strident and partisan support. The UPC Congress had an official party newspaper, The People as well as The Nationalist and in the Luganda language Njuba. The DP had two magazines, Point and Exposure, as well as The Citizen, The Champion, The Star and The Economy and five weeklies in Uganda. The UPM was supported by Topic, perhaps the most intellectually stimulating publication in the country, The Equator which sometimes appeared bi-weekly, The Pilot and at least one Luganda language paper Ssekanyolya. Even the newly formed CP had the Kampala Guardian. And for the faithful who wished to have their political news from the Church, there was the New Century published by the Church of Uganda.[15]

Length of the Campaign. The campaign should be long enough that any disadvantaged parties--disadvantaged by virtue of having been previously banned or in exile--have the opportunity to fully organize and actively put their message to the voters. Complete equity in this matter is often impossible since the party affiliated with the antecedent state(s) will have had, in effect, years of campaign experience and organization behind it. Nevertheless, once the plebiscite zone has been fully neutralized and pacified, the electoral roll compiled and verified,and the party organizations brought up to reasonably full strength, a campaign of three weeks has been found to be adequate.

SYMBOLS

Symbols play a significant role in most competitive election campaigns. Flags, banners, emblems--even songs and dances--are instrumental to the efforts of the parties to demonstrate the depth and breadth of commitment to their respective causes. Symbols also serve to reawaken deeply held values and commitments that underpin the choices made by voters at the polls.

The use of symbols, routine in most domestic elections, is a recipe for conflict in a plebiscite. A plebiscite is an opportunity for the participants to proclaim their national pride and cultural identity. The pride that a people hold for their history, language, and traditions is invested in symbols of nationhood: a national flag, national colors, national emblems, a national anthem. However, when one nationality is ruled by a state controlled by another nation, the symbols of the ruling nation (and the ruling nation's state) often become the hated symbols of oppression. To the ruling nation, any display of the symbols of the subject nation is evidence of disloyalty and treachery.

Each plebiscite regime must assess the conflict potential of the symbols likely to be employed by the parties to a plebiscite. Where national antipathies are at a low to moderate degree of intensity, plebiscite commissions have permitted the wearing of small emblems and the display of flags from buildings if placed above the ground floor. In conditions of intense animosity, such as in Upper Silesia, the display of all flags (except those of the plebiscite commission and of diplomatic missions) or emblems was prohibited. The singing of national songs was prohibited to groups of over twenty persons.[16]

> In December 1934 the Governing Commission in the Saar prohibited the public display of all national flags, or flags or banners bearing the colors of the Saar Territory or of towns in the Territory, the colors of churches, or banners or symbols which had a special political character in connection with the plebiscite.[17]

Even so, the Deutsche Front, the official group campaigning for the immediate reunion of the Saar with Germany, successfully circumvented the intent of the

Commission by instructing its followers to remove their flags

> but to hang on each empty flagpole a bunch of Christmas greens as a symbol, to festoon each house with garlands, and--contrary to Saar custom--to place a Christmas candle in each window as a special demonstration.[18]

The opposition, those favoring a continuation of the status quo, immediately instructed its followers to do likewise. Thus, the people of the Saar celebrated their most decorative Christmas--if not their most political.

ELECTORAL INTIMIDATION

The greatest threat to a plebiscite is electoral intimidation. Coercive threats undermine democracy for the same reason that they subvert contracts: the element of free choice is nullified. Electoral intimidation is uncommon in domestic elections for two reasons. First, the people of most stable, multi-party democracies accept the rules of the electoral game and will stand behind the winner of the election whether or not they voted for him. Intimidation is almost wholely absent in such conditions. Second, in states with openly rigged or one-party elections in which the voter is presented no choice between potential winners and losers, electoral intimidation is also largely absent. (Intimidation comes into play only if the voter wishes to abstain from voting in a conspicuous manner because failure to vote may be interpreted as a lack of loyalty to the regime.) Hence, the voter in a ruthless dictatorship is seldom a victim of electoral intimidation on voting day. Rather, he is a year-around victim of political coercion designed to constrain his ability to participate meaningfully in civic affairs. Thus, electoral intimidation is a characteristic of open, competitive elections held in uncertain and unstable conditions.

Fear and anxiety concerning the outcome of elections is an unavoidable element of competitive elections by virtue of the fact that there ARE winners and losers. Indeed, politics itself (i.e., the authoritative allocation of values) is about winning and losing. The point of a competitive election is that the decision over who wins and loses is taken at the polls rather than behind closed doors--or on the battlefield. For an election to be meaningful--to decide who gets what, when, where--there must be the prospect of at least relative gains and losses. A successful electoral process keeps the losers "on board" by containing the losses suffered by the losers to a level acceptable to the losers--and to the winners. There are several kinds of losses that are clearly unacceptable in most circumstances: (1) A loss of personal safety, e.g., threats of violence. (2) A loss of participatory rights, e.g., the right to vote, speak, hold office. (3) A severe loss of economic opportunities, e.g., loss of the right to pursue one's occupation, confiscation of one's assets. (4) A loss of basic cultural institutions, e.g., the closing of one's churches or schools.

Persons who are threatened with the loss of any of the above if they fail to vote "correctly" are potential victims of electoral intimidation. This is not to say that the contestants in an election cannot paint a bleak picture of what might happen should the other side win. Bishop Abel Muzorewa, charging that a ZANU (PF) or PF victory would bring Mozambique-style repression to Zimbabwe, declared:

> In Mozambique the people are literally dying of starvation . . . if ZANU (PF) or the PF are allowed to impose the same kind of government upon us you will lose your house, your land, your cattle, goats and chickens . . . your children will be taken away . . . [and] taught to hate the ways of their parents and their tribe . . . to hate both God and the ancestral spirits. Machel is now vomiting this kind of government, why do ZANU (PF) and the PF want us to eat other people's vomit?[19]

Such heated campaign rhetoric is testimony to the fact that an election may be the genuine article--that the voter's choice will have a real impact on the course of events. Ethnic groups, classes, or regions can lose their predominance through elections. Wealth, status, and positions of power may be redistributed. Either such things will be done by the voters through the ballot box or they will be done by juntas or self-appointed wisemen behind locked doors. Bishop Muzorewa's statement was a warning to the people of Zimbabwe. It was not an act of electoral intimidation since it was directed to the people of Zimbabwe as a whole and not at specific individuals or groups in Zimbabwe.

Guarding Against Electoral Intimidation

It is the responsibility of a plebiscite regime to insure that the inhabitants of a plebiscite zone have the opportunity to discuss and ponder the gains and losses that the various outcomes of the plebiscite may entail. A free and open campaign conducted in an atmosphere of sobriety and tranquility is thereby essential. Acts of overt intimidation or pointed threats of reprisal occur in most plebiscites--given the emotional power of national and sovereignty issues. To keep such acts from poisoning the validity of the plebiscite, the Plebiscite Commission must take firm measures to safeguard the lives and property of all the zone's inhabitants. At every phase of the plebiscite the state and non-state parties to the plebiscite must reiterate their refusal to sanction reprisals in the post-plebiscite era.

The Plebiscite Commission can take several concrete steps to lessen the danger of intimidation:
(1) All troops (regular or irregular) except the Commission's own neutral troops must be kept inside their bases and assembly areas.
(2) The local police should, where possible, be disarmed and in all events be entirely neutralized.
(3) The use of threats against persons or groups in speeches, posters, or publications must be strictly prohibited. Pictures or symbols portraying weapons of all kinds should be banned. Lord Soames describes the firm action he took to deal with campaign intimidation in the Zimbabwe-Rhodesia (1980) election:

> On February 5 I took powers to enable me to suspend an individual from taking part in the election campaign, or to suspend a party from campaigning in a particular area, or to suspend all campaigning in a given area. And on February 12 I took the power to exclude an area from the election altogether if I was satisfied that it was impossible to conduct a free and fair election campaign there. I took action subsequently to exclude one candidate from the election campaign--although he was not prevented from standing--and to suspend one party from campaigning in two small districts. This action

> naturally exposed me to a cross-fire from opposite directions. On the one hand I was blamed for going too far, and on the other for not going far enough. The pressures from both sides were intense. But again I believe in retrospect that the action I took was broadly right. I am satisfied that the pressure of intimidation on the electorate eased in the closing stages of the campaign--let others argue whether this was propter hoc and not merely post hoc. And--most important of all--in the event no party withdrew from the election on the ground that it had been placed at an unacceptable disadvantage by intimidation by others.[20]

(4) The absolute secrecy of the balloting procedure should be reinforced to the public through an intensive publicity campaign. The fact that the ballots will be mixed so that no neighborhood or village's vote can be known should be stressed.
(5) Neutral observers should be present in significant numbers and should be highly visible to the populace.
(6) The generous size of the post-plebiscite economic aid package pledged by states and international organizations should be publicized.
(7) A rumor control center should be established. Equipped with radios and aircraft, rumor control teams must be dispatched quickly to check-out rumors and to broadcast the truth. Such centers, developed in a number of American cities in response to inner city riots, provide both an early warning of dangerous rumors and the capacity to squelch rumors quickly. Rumors have an unfailing propensity to crop-up on election eve and on voting day. If voters cast their ballots even partially on the basis of rumors that are later discredited, the legitimacy of the vote is tainted.

Crime, banditry, and personal vendettas will occur during plebiscites as they do at all times. However, such acts may mistakenly acquire political connotations and become the source of frightful rumors. Hence, rapid and thorough investigation of all crimes of violence must be conducted and the results quickly publicized.

Charges of intimidation lodged by the parties to a plebiscite should also be checked-out quickly. The Commonwealth Observer Group in Zimbabwe-Rhodesia noted:

> In the course of our examination, it became apparent to us that many of the parties who were complaining of an inability to campaign in certain areas had simply not tried to do so. Others had pleaded intimidation as the cause for people failing to attend their meetings rather than concede that they had no following there. Intimidation had become the catch-cry of the campaign, and it was echoed time and again.[21]

Electoral intimidation is a complex phenomenon that has been largely ignored by scholars. The above mentioned Commonwealth Observer Group found that "no ready reference works are available on the subject."[22] It is surprising that so little research has been conducted on a problem that is so threatening to fledgling democracies around the world.

NEUTRAL OBSERVERS

Groups of independent, neutral observers--unconnected to the Plebiscite Commission--can play an important role in a plebiscite. They are an additional source of external validation. While their task is to observe, not to supervise, they should be more than passive bystanders. The Commonwealth Observer Group in Zimbabwe-Rhodesia (1980) took a characteristically active part.

> . . . we travelled extensively, in small groups that based themselves in each provincial office by turn. To underline the collective nature of our responsibilities and to neutralise any possible suggestion that particular national tendencies might have affected the process of our observation, each group was so mixed as to consist of not less than four and at times as many as eight different nationalities. This helped each of us impartially to observe the election campaign and assess the mood of the public in different parts of the country. Periodically we assembled in Salisbury to exchange observations as a group. Our programme was kept flexible, allowing us to concentrate attention on areas which required special investigation from time to time. The decentralisation of our operations made possible

a great deal of independent travel, and was vital for the effective coverage of polling stations at the time of the elections.

We went to a large number of the Tribal Trust Lands (TTLs) in which one fourth of the African population of Rhodesia lives. We visited urban areas, African townships, protected villages, government offices, cease-fire assembly places, army and Auxiliary force bases, police camps, refugee centres, national crossing points, schools, hospitals, missions, prisons and detention centres, and major concentrations of employees at factories, mines and commercial farms. We talked to people on urban streets and by rural roadsides, in bars, shops and market places. We visited each of the country's 55 administrative districts, many several times.[23]

Neutral observers can influence the course of a plebiscite by means of gentle pressure and persuasion. However, an observer group can also brandish a formidable weapon--the threat to withdraw. Such a threat--a rare event indeed--was made by the Commonwealth Observer Group in Uganda (1980). It was issued in a letter sent by the Group's chairman, Mr. E.M. Debrah, to the chairman of the Ugandan government's Military Commission, Mr. Paulo Muwanga.

12 December 1980

My Dear Chairman,

We came to observe elections and, as our interim report shows, were impressed by the poll. That you have succeeded in holding free and fair elections in the most unlikely of environments has been an outstanding achievement. We cannot hide our dismay at the possibility that this entire noble enterprise may now miscarry. We know much of what took place at the polls and the count from our physical presence at polling stations in almost every district of Uganda and shall, of course, deal with these in our final report.

In view of last night's proclamation, and the fact that we have now been denied access to the Electoral Commission we are now considering whether we can serve any useful purpose by remaining here. By our mandate we must work within the laws of Uganda, and these have now been altered so as to make continuation of our task impossible.

Even at this late stage, it is our urgent plea that for the good of Uganda, the position be reconsidered and the verdict of the people be respected. We are sure you will appreciate that if the results are to be believed, the final stages of the counting must be carried out in an open manner, and the normal channels of the courts kept open.

We urge you, with all the conviction at our command and with the best interests of the people of Uganda at heart, to permit us to resume our task and to ensure that the incoming government will be accorded an honoured place amongst nations committed to the democratic process.

Sincerely yours,
E.M. Debrah
Chairman[24]

Adjustments were soon made that permitted the observers to carry-on with their work.

The ideal observer is a person who speaks the native languages, is familiar from first-hand experience with the nuts and bolts of election procedures in his home country, and who is not linked in any important manner to any of the principal parties to the plebiscite. It is usually a mistake to send former ambassadors or foreign service personnel who have served in adjacent countries. They will be viewed, rightly or wrongly, as being in the camp of the countries in which they were posted. Celebrities of all sorts tend to make poor observers given the fundamentally unglamorous and low-profile character of the job. Academics from small colleges, given their foreign language and research skills, have been shown to make good observers.

FOREIGN PRESS

The foreign press also serve a useful role as observers of the conduct of a plebiscite. They are valuable for several reasons above and beyond their role as communicators to the outside world. The presence of foreign journalists with their cameras and recording equipment are a major deterrent to attempts at intimidation. When incidents do occur, it is the victim and the victim's cause that receive the principal media play. Secondly, the foreign press interacts frequently with the local administration and police--securing permits, arranging transport and communications, seeking information. By doing so the press assists in the supervision of local officials. Thirdly, foreign journalists often bring to the press conferences of the various parties to a plebiscite a skepticism and a directness that would otherwise be lacking. Officials, accustomed to a thoroughly cowed local media, are often dramatically deflated. Guerrilla leaders, accustomed only to addressing their troops and other devotees, may beat a disorderly retreat.

Fourthly, the foreign media plays a vital role in the spiking of rumors. Gregory tells of the quashing of the "Coca Cola" rumor during the Zimbabwe-Rhodesia election.

> Potentially the most serious allegation was that by use of liquids ranging from Coca Cola to paint thinner some people had managed to remove from their hands the invisible dye which was used to detect attempts to vote twice. This allegation was conclusively refuted by the Election Commissioner, Sir John Boynton, in a practical demonstration arranged by him in Salisbury in front of scores of journalists and observers.[25]

Foreign journalists, possessing a credibility lacked by the local journalists, accepted the Election Commissioner's refutation and quickly set the rumor to rest.

Finally, the fact that the eyes of the world are focused upon a plebiscite is brought home to the local people by the presence of foreign journalists. The seriousness of the plebiscite is thus underlined for the people whose destiny is at stake.

PUBLIC OPINION POLLING

Should public opinion polls be permitted during the conduct of a plebiscite? This question is not unique to plebiscites. It is asked in most democracies today where public opinion polling has become an important part of political life. The polls are criticized not so much for their accuracy--the polls often have a sound track record for accuracy--as for the way in which they shape perceptions of the campaign. A candidate or party that does poorly in the polls early in a campaign is often "written off" as a loser. As a result, endorsements are withheld, media attention is diverted elsewhere, volunteer workers melt away or switch to more highly rated candidates or parties.

The publication of opinion polls can become the main "events" of an election campaign. For example, polling results were the largest single type of "news" in the 1983 British General Election. Nearly every day the press and the electronic media published the results of new polls and then filled the newspapers and the air waves with the reactions of candidates and party leaders to the polls. Thus, some argue that opinion polls distract the public from the real issues of a campaign.

Nevertheless, few countries have followed the example of France which in 1977 prohibited the publication of polling results during a period beginning one week before the first round of a general election and continuing until the run-off vote (the second round) is completed.[26] The view is widely held that people will always speculate on the fortunes of candidates and parties during election campaigns. Hence, it is thought that there is little harm done if the speculation is more scientifically based. Others stress the importance of freedom of speech and of the press in democratic societies--especially during election campaigns. The banning of opinion polls would therefore be an unhealthy infringement of the fundamental rights that underpin democratic life.

Plebiscites are significantly different from the elections routinely conducted in democratic states. Plebiscites are extraordinary events. They typically occur at times and in places of bitter discord. Often they take place in countries without a tradition of competitive elections. Thus, the conditions in which plebiscites are typically held are often not conducive to public opinion sampling.

As discussed earlier, intimidation is a paramount

threat to the successful conduct of a plebiscite. The essential defense against threats of violence during the run-up to the election and of reprisals after the vote is to safeguard the secrecy of the voter's decision. This requires more than a secret ballot. The voter must be protected from attempts to force him to reveal his voting intention before the election is held. An illustration from the Saar plebiscite of 1935 will make this clear.

The Deutsche Front, the official organization in the Saar campaigning for reunification with Germany, initiated a drive to encourage pro-Germany householders to place signs in their windows. The signs read:

LOYALTY IS THE MARK OF HONOR.
THE LAND BECOMES FREE AND THE MORNING DAWNS.

Or, coming directly to the point:

ON JANUARY 13 I WILL VOTE FOR GERMANY.

The Plebiscite Commission uncovered unmistakable evidence that the Deutsche Front, an arm of Hitler's National Socialist Party, was threatening reprisals against those householders who failed to display the signs.[27]

It was to cover situations such as this that the Plebiscite Commission in the Saar had enacted a statute that prohibited any person from unlawfully seeking "to influence any other person to reveal the manner in which he proposed to vote."[28] Thus, the Commission sought to prevent situations in which pressure was placed upon voters to reveal publicly their voting intention. For this reason, many of the plebiscites conducted in this century have banned or restricted the display of flags and signs or the wearing of badges.

Seen in this light, public opinion polling can cause problems. Valid polling requires the voter to disclose his voting intention. At best, an opinion sample taken in circumstances of possible intimidation is likely to place the voter in an uncomfortable position. At worst, the taking of a poll can be the occasion for pressure and intimidation by partisans of the various sides. In point of fact, there are no reports of scientifically designed opinion polls being taken in the plebiscites of this century. There is one instance of an opinion poll reported by Gregory that was purportedly conducted during the internationally supervised election in Zimbabwe-Rhodesia in 1980.

> The one opinion poll that was published during the election campaign, by the pro-Muzorewa National Observer newspaper, proved to be completely unreliable. Conducted by an unnamed 'international market research company' and claiming that the 'methods used were those of the Gallup Poll,' the 'opinion test' detected a massive shift of support away from ZANU (PF). The poll predicted that Bishop Muzorewa's United African National Council (UANC) would win the largest number of seats.[29]

In the event, Robert Mugabe's ZANU (PF) rolled to a landslide victory with nearly 63% of the vote (and two thirds of the seats) compared to Bishop Muzorewa's U.A.N.C. which took only 8% of the vote.

In sum, unless the danger of intimidation has been completely removed, public opinion polling should probably be prohibited or restricted in most plebiscites.

BALLOTS AND BALLOT BOXES

A ballot paper must be designed so that it is clearly understandable to the voter, that the voter's decision be kept totally secret, that the ballot cannot be forged, and that the voter's decision recorded on the ballot is univocally clear to the counting officials. Given the human race's unlimited potential for ingenuity and deviousness, the secure accomplishment of such design tasks can be extraordinarily difficult. It is doubly difficult because these tasks must not only be accomplished but must be seen and believed to have been accomplished. Thus, no amount of rigor can be spared on the printing, transportation, distribution, marking, collecting, counting, and ultimate disposal of ballot papers.

For the post-World War One plebiscites, a multiple ballot paper and envelope system was developed. Each voter would receive one ballot for each option, e.g., in Schleswig, one ballot paper for Germany and one for Denmark. In the secrecy of the polling booth, the voter would place his favored ballot in an official envelope. The rejected ballot would be torn-up by the voter and also placed into the envelope. The envelope was then put into the ballot box. This system proved very effective and virtually tamper-proof. One advantage is that no marking of the ballot is necessary. No pens or pencils are used and there are no controversies when a voter's mark is unclear or indistinct. Such ballot papers are of particular value when there are large numbers of illiterate or semi-literate voters. Each ballot is usually of a different color and contains on it the flag or symbol--as well as the words--indicating the option.

The innovation of requiring that the ballot paper for the rejected option be enclosed in the envelope emerged when some voters in Upper Silesia--where this was not done--were threatened with violence if they could not produce the rejected ballot to prove they had voted "correctly." Other voters were offered cash in exchange for their unused ballots.[30]

Ballot papers should be printed by a reputable firm of security printers and should have the same sort of complex design as bank notes. If the multiple ballot paper system is used, the ballots for each option should be on paper of identical quality and thickness. The need for such rigorous attention to detail was highlighted in the Sopron plebiscite (1921) where the Austrian ballot papers were thicker than the Hungarian ballot papers. Thus by listening carefully, an observer standing outside the polling booth could tell which ballot paper was being torn up.[31] The Saar plebiscite commission kept the color of the ballot papers a secret for as long as possible to hinder attempts at forgery. As a further check on forgery, various stamps and perforating devices have been used to assure that the ballots handed to the voters are the ones that end up in the ballot boxes. The strictest security should be exercised over the ballot papers before the vote with regular inspections to determine if any have been stolen. Such a theft did occur prior to the Zimbabwe-Rhodesia (1980) election.

> In fact, one pad of 200 papers for Manicaland was stolen from the Government Printer, but the theft was promptly revealed by the elaborate system of cross-checks developed by HMSO, which had one of its staff supervising the printing. Although the theft could not have affected the ballot, the Election Commissioner arranged for a new set of ballot papers to be produced for Manicaland printed on a green paper and the old ones destroyed.[32]

Ballot Boxes

In an era of mechanical and electronic gadgets it may seem antediluvian to use ballot papers and ballot boxes. Nevertheless, it is a technique for voting that has withstood a century of testing. (Some even claim that the technique provides psychic rewards that machine voting cannot achieve, e.g., the sense of accomplishment and of finality when one thrusts the ballot into the slot atop the ballot box.) The technique of voting with ballot and ballot box has the virtue of simplicity and, with constant vigilance, can be made to work anywhere in the world.

The ballot box (or "voting urn" as much of the world calls it) can be made secure in several ways. All boxes should be thoroughly inspected to verify their emptiness before the polls open. The structural integrity of each box must be checked--a precaution often ignored. Damaging rumors commonly arise to the effect that there are hidden cracks or secret holes in ballot boxes that are used to rig the vote. The 1980 Zimbabwe-Rhodesia vote produced one such rumor.

> Rumours still circulated from the April 1979 elections that it was possible to introduce additional ballot papers to sealed ballot boxes by removing the wooden handles from their sides. Our investigations revealed that this would be quite impossible. The handles were not set into the wooden sides of the boxes, but fixed on to the outside by means of two screws. Were a handled to be removed (and as the screw was placed through from the inside of the boxes this would itself present difficulties) one would simply be confronted with two small screw holes through which it would be exceedingly difficult to introduce a ballot paper. We were satisfied with the construction of the boxes.[33]

Hence, ballot boxes should be checked by agents of the Plebiscite Commission, representatives of the parties, neutral outside observers, and journalists to certify their structural integrity and to spike rumors to the contrary.

POLLING STATIONS

The polling station is the focal point of the plebiscite. It is where the eligible voter is officially identified and where the voter's decision is officially recorded.

If a plebiscite zone has recent experience in holding elections, the distribution of polling stations in the most recent election is a good first approximation. In any event, a study should be made in which catchment areas for polling stations are assessed in terms of (1) numbers of likely voters, (2) pedestrian and vehicle transit time to and from polling stations, and (3) the expected flow rate of voters through the polling stations. Finally, (4) the security situation must be evaluated and correlated with the resources available to insure the safety of the polling stations.

(1) Recent census returns and the Plebiscite Commission's own voter registration lists should enable researchers to map the distribution and density of eligible voters in the plebiscite zone. In cases where war or revolution have dislocated significant portions of the population, guestimates must be made. Mobile polling stations can add a needed element of flexibility in such situations. It is far wiser to have too many polling stations than too few. The Zimbabwe-Rhodesia election (1980) is instructive on this matter since years of fighting had made population estimates unreliable and there was no attempt at voter registration.

> For example, when one of us arrived at Jichedza in Ndanga District we found about 7,000 people waiting to vote at a mobile scheduled to stay for only a further four hours. In many parts of the country, mobiles fell well behind schedule in this way owing to underestimation of the numbers who would be voting.[34]

(2) The transit time for voters to reach the polling stations and to return home must be calculated on a worst case basis. In much of the world rain closes roads and public transportation cannot be relied upon--or may be sabotaged. Hence, pessimistic assumptions should underpin transit time estimates. Modern computer mapping techniques can be of considerable use in producing such estimates.

(3) The flow rate of voters through the polling stations can be estimated by the use of simulations. The simulated polling station, like the real ones, will process voters according to (a) its physical lay-out, and (b) the voting drill and the proficiency of the polling officials at performing the voting drill.

(a) The physical lay-out of the polling station requires some attention. If possible, guidelines should be developed that will insure a minimally acceptable flow rate. The Commonwealth Observer Group in Uganda (1980) pointed to the importance of the lay-out.

> Polling stations were located in a variety of settings. Some were in schools, some in government offices, some in the open air. Some were sheltered under verandahs, some under thatched canopies. A number of polling stations we visited were ill-suited for the flow of people at the rate required. Some used the entrance door also as an exit. Others had the ballot boxes in a separate room with two doors so that a person waiting to enter the room to vote had no idea how long he should wait or whether the person ahead of him had long since left the booth. In one polling station voters had to use a window as their exit. Despite physical difficulties, the voting proceeded surprisingly smoothly.[35]

The Ugandan Electoral Commission's initial estimate of an average processing time of 36 seconds per voter was viewed as unrealistic by the Observer Group. They recommended that the polling stations be kept open for additional hours.

The selection of suitable buildings to be used as polling stations must be done with some care.

> In Yap, one or two polling stations were situated in "men's houses," which are traditionally barred to women, but the Mission was assured that the tradition had been relaxed for elections and did indeed witness women voting without difficulty at such stations.[36]

(b) The other determinant of the flow rate is the complexity of the voting drill and the proficiency of the polling officials in executing the drill. The voting drill used in the 1980 Zimbabwe-Rhodesia election is a good recent illustration.

VOTING DRILL

1. The presiding officer will regulate the number of voters to be admitted to a polling station at any one time.
2. The voter will be identified as a person eligible to receive a ballot paper before being admitted to a polling station. Voters will have been instructed to take to the polling station whatever personal documents they may have in order to establish identity and eligibility.
   The presiding officer may or may not call for such documents but in the event of his being in any doubt as to the right of any person to receive a ballot paper he is empowered to insist upon documentary evidence. (Section 175 (10)(b)).
3. On admission to the polling station the voter, who may only vote once at an election, will be directed to the checking device in which he or she will place each hand palm downwards. (Section 175 (10)(a) and (Section 62 (4)(a)).
4. If the checking device reveals that the voter has already voted in the election a ballot paper will not be issued and the person concerned will be requested to leave the polling station. (Section 62 (4)(a)).
5. If the checking device reveals that the voter has not previously voted in the election he or she will be requested to dip the fingers of both hands into the invisible marking fluid. (Section 62 (4)(b)).
6 A polling officer will perforate the ballot paper in the top right-hand corner to obliterate the serial number with the perforating machine which will be used at this election in lieu of a secret mark which was previously the practice. Once the paper has been perforated the polling officer will hand it to the voter. (Section 63 (L)(b)).
7. The voter will be directed to a polling booth where, in complete privacy and secrecy, the ballot paper will be marked with an X against

the name of the political party of his or her choice.
Before leaving the polling booth the voter will fold the ballot paper so that the official mark of the polling station is visible but the names of the political parties and cross made by him or her is not visible. (Section 63 (1)(c)).

8. Having marked and folded the ballot paper as set out above the voter is required to drop the ballot paper into the ballot box displaying to the presiding officer or polling officer in attendance the official mark of the polling station but NOT the manner in which the voter has cast his vote. (Section 63 (1)(c)).
9. The voter will then leave the polling station.
10. If a voter inadvertently spoils a ballot paper before dropping it into the ballot box he or she may surrender it to the presiding officer who will issue a new ballot paper and endorse the surrendered ballot paper as "cancelled."
Ballot papers surrendered in these circumstances will be made up into a separate packet by the presiding officer at the close of poll. The packet will be labelled "spoilt ballot papers surrendered" and will be endorsed with the number of papers contained therein. (Section 64).
11. At the request, in person, of a voter who cannot read or write or who is incapable by blindness or other physical cause from voting in the manner set out in paragraphs 1 to 8 above, the presiding officer shall mark the vote of that voter on the ballot paper in the manner directed by the voter and place it in the ballot box.
If the instructions of the voter as to the manner in which the presiding officer is to make his vote on the ballot paper are not sufficiently clear to enable the presiding officer to make the vote, the presideing officer may put such questions to the voter as he considers necessary to enable him to do so. (Section 175 (11)).

All references are to the Electoral Act No. 14 of 1979.

E.W. Pope-Simmonds
Registrar-General of Elections[37]

Clearly, the flow rate will depend upon the training of the polling station officials. Even so, unique problems will arise that cannot be resolved satisfactorally by the local polling staff. Hence, it is desirable that telephone or radio communication facilities be available linking the polling stations with the headquarters of the Plebiscite Commission. Such linkage will reduce the chance of local or regional interpretations of the voting regulations being developed--and producing bitter controversy after the vote.

Official agents of the parties to a plebiscite are typically attached to each polling station. By closely watching the work of the polling officials--and each other--they act as guarantors of the integrity of the vote. Before the polls open, the party agents should verify the number of ballots issued to the polling station and check to see that the ballot boxes are empty and properly locked. In some elections the party agents are invited to place their own seals on the boxes. If the voting takes place over several days, the agents may guard the ballot boxes--and each other--at night. Following the final closure of the polls, the party agents should reconcile the number of ballot papers that were used and those that were not used against the original number issued to the polling station.[38] The agents may also accompany the ballot boxes to the counting centers and observe the count. In sum, the party agents are a basic "check and balance" in the voting system and no polling station is complete without them.

(4) In unsettled conditions where the danger of intimidation or violent disruption exists, the number and location of polling stations must be tailored to the security resources of the Plebiscite Commission. If the armed presence of neutral troops is the only way to keep order on voting day, the vote should probably be delayed. If the danger comes only from a few extremists or renegades, the vote can be organized on a staggered basis. The regions of the plebiscite zone can hold their vote on different days--allowing the bulk of the neutral troops and other security personnel to move from region to region to safeguard the polling stations, officials, and voters.

VOTING DAY

Voting day has a special, almost magical quality. It is an improbable sort of day--a day when some of mankind's most devisive conflicts face the prospect of peaceful resolution. The political temperature, raised by the campaign, suddenly falls. Especially for peoples who have suffered years of bloodshed and strife, voting day means hope--hope for the security of a just peace.

In the wake of a free and open campaign conducted in a proper, plebiscitary atmosphere, voting day is usually quiet. Typically held on a Sunday or a special holiday, only a few precautions need be taken. Traditionally, alcohol sales are banned and the bars are closed. Often, joint declarations signed by all the party leaders are circulated widely in the media. The party leaders in Uganda (1980) issued the following statement:

JOINT DECLARATION BY LEADERS

> During the past eight years the people of Uganda have suffered grievously. Many lives have been lost, the economy devastated and we have endured both personal and national humiliation. For us to embark successfully on the process of rebuilding and revitalising our nation, all of us recognise as essential our parties' commitment to the democratic process--a process which alone carries a guarantee that our human rights and freedom will never again be circumscribed.
>
> Each of us leads a party committed to campaigning peacefully and without intimidation. Each of us calls upon all the persons who support us to desist from any activities designed to influence voting by threats or force. We call upon them to desist from interference with the ability of other parties to campaign freely and to put their case to the electorate.
>
> As leaders of our respective parties we assure all Ugandans that the ballot is secret and that voters should vote without fear for the party of their choice.

> Whatever our differences, we are at one in our pledge to serve Uganda and all her people.[39]

Other declarations may be broadcast--this one telegraphed by the Council of the League of Nations to the people of the Saar:

> On the eve of the plebiscite, the Council desires to make a solemn appeal to the population of the Saar.
>
> It urges them to show by their calm and dignified attitude that they are conscious of the importance of the vote which they are called upon to record.
>
> It counts upon their preserving the same attitude after the vote and awaiting with confidence the decisions which the Council will take within as short an interval as possible following upon the vote.[40]

The presence of large numbers of foreign journalists and of neutral observer groups tends to make the voter conscious of the fact that the world's spotlight has been focused upon him. It is this sense of occasion that underlies the serious tone of most plebiscite voting days.

VOTE COUNTING

The count begins with the accounting of all ballots used and unused at each polling station and ends with the certification of the vote by the Vote Contest Board. If there is adequate security, an important step in the accounting or "reconciliation" process may be carried-out in the polling station. In this procedure, the ballot boxes are opened and the ballots (or ballot envelopes) are counted face down. Thus, the exact number of ballots in each box may be ascertained and squared with the number issued to voters. It may be desireable to package the ballots into bundles and to seal the bundles before replacing them into their respective ballot boxes. The boxes are then relocked, sealed, and transported under armed guard to the central counting bureau.

The first task of the central (or regional) counting bureau, after verifying the seals, is to open each box and perform another face down count. The number should equal the number counted at the polling station. The next step is to mix the ballots from boxes in the same voting district--thereby protecting the anonymity of neighborhoods and villages.[41] Access to the counting hall must be strictly limited to plebiscite officials, accredited party agents, neutral observers, and accredited journalists. All persons entering the hall should be searched to keep the plebiscite from being sabotaged at the last minute by a bomb.

Counting may then proceed in the normal fashion--creating one hundred ballot stacks and so forth. Invalid ballots are those where (a) the intention of the voter cannot be determined with certainty, (b) there is evidence of the identity of the voter, and (c) the ballot paper appears to be a forgery. A special file must be made of all invalid votes in which the ballot itself and the written reasons for the ballot's invalidity are included.

There are unaccountable irregularities in all elections. The standard to be applied is not that of perfection but the standard achieved by other free elections. Voters will put ballots in their pockets and walk away. Others will place their ballots under the ballot boxes instead of in them. Counting clerks will miscount. The only answer is constant supervision at the polling stations and in the counting bureaus and frequent counting and recounting.

The Plebiscite Commission should not let itself be rushed into announcing a preliminary result but should act before rumors of the result take-on a life of their own. It must be stressed that vote totals are preliminary pending certification by the Vote Contest Board.

A period of one week should be designated for the receipt of charges of voting irregularities. Another week should suffice for the Vote Contest Board to investigate the charges and reach a determination of the validity of the overall vote. (It should be recalled that the function of the Vote Contest Board is not the protection of individual rights but the certification of the poll.)

An illustration of the kind of irregularities that require investigation is provided by the United Nations Visiting Mission that observed the 1978 referendum in the Trust Territory of the Pacific Islands:

> The complaints fell into two broad categories: improprieties in election procedure and improper campaign practices. The chief allegations in the first category made by the complainants supporting the constitution were

listed as follows in the Chairman's letter to Congress enclosing the Hamilton report.

(a) Ineligible persons were allowed to vote;
(b) Numerous Palauans living in Guam were improperly refused registration;
(c) Some 800 absentee ballots were mishandled, raising the possibility of ballot tampering;
(d) Certain ballots bore duplicate numbers, suggesting that forgery had occurred;
(e) Around 750 to 800 votes were not counted;
(f) Forty-five more ballots were returned from the island of Angaur than were sent it.

The Special Joint Committee concluded that only the first of these complaints had substance. Twenty-five affidavits by absentee voters living in Guam proved to belong to United States citizens who had improperly been allowed to vote . . . Mr. Hamilton pointed out in his report that the existence of 25 improper ballots does not, standing alone, invalidate an election where the margin of victory was 619 votes.[42]

NOTES

[1]Sarah Wambaugh, Plebiscites Since the World War (Washington, D.C.: Carnegie Endowment for International Peace, 1933), pp. 224; 239.

[2]Sarah Wambaugh, The Saar Plebiscite (Cambridge: Harvard University Press, 1940), pp. 172-173.

[3]Wambaugh, Saar, p. 242.

[4]Wambaugh, Saar, p. 235.

[5]Colin Baker, "Conducting the Elections in Zimbabwe 1980," Public Administration and Development, Vol. 2, No. 1 (January-March 1983), p. 49.

[6]Baker, p. 49.

[7]Baker, p. 50. The use of dyes or inks is a common practice. An illustration from the Mariana Islands: "As an anti-fraud measure, a bottle of indelible ink ("Dr. Palacios' Magic Brew") was made available at each polling place; if the polling judges deemed it necessary, the registered voter, after casting his vote, was asked to dip his left hand index finger in the ink to prevent his voting again in a different precinct." Report of the United Nations Visiting Mission to Observe the Plebiscite

in the Mariana Islands District, Trust Territory of the Pacific Islands, June 1975. New York: United Nations, T/1771.

[8]Wambaugh, Plebiscites, p. 77.

[9]General Lassiter quoted in Wambaugh, Plebiscites, p. 383. The role of the outvoter remains controversial. "An associate justice of the Palau Supreme Court has barred certification of the plebiscite results [of February 10, 1983] until a lawsuit charging voting irregularities is heard this week. . . The lawsuit, brought by a Palauan senator and several other people, objects to off-island ballots." Robert Trumbull, "Palau, U.S. Officials to Discuss Islands' Vote," International Herald Tribune, February 23, 1983, p. 5.

[10]Wambaugh, Saar, p. 217.

[11]Wambaugh, Plebiscites, p. 84.

[12]Wambaugh, Plebiscites, p. 190.

[13]Southern Rhodesia Elections: February, 1980. The Report of the Commonwealth Observer Group on elections leading to independent Zimbabwe (London: Commonwealth Secretariat, 1980). p. 214.

[14]Wambaugh, Plebiscites, p. 14.

[15]Uganda Elections: December, 1980. The Report of the Commonwealth Observer Groups (London: Commonwealth Secretariat, 1980), pp. 18-19. In the 1979 Marshall Islands referendum: "As was the case in the 1978 referendum, the radio was by far the most important medium for information during the campaign preceding the 1979 referendum. Equal radio time was allotted to each side for political broadcasts during the campaign and, although The Voice of the Marshalls complained to the Mission of discrimination, in fact, neither side took up the full time available to it." Report of the United Nations Visiting Mission to Observe the Referendum in the Marshall Islands, Trust Territory of the Pacific Islands, March 1979. New York: United Nations, T/1805.

[16]Wambaugh, Plebiscites, p. 233.

[17]Wambaugh, Saar, p. 281.

[18]Wambaugh, Saar, p. 286.

[19]Martin Gregory, "Zimbabwe 1980: Politicisation through Armed Struggle and Electoral Mobilisation," Journal of Commonwealth and Comparative Politics, Vol. XIX, No. 1 (March 1981), p. 82.

[20]Lord Soames, "From Rhodesia to Zimbabwe," International Affairs, Vol. 56, No. 3 (Summer 1980). p. 415. The 1956 Togoland Plebiscite produced an unusual case of intimidation. "Mention should perhaps be made of

the one conviction under section 40 of the Plebiscite Regulations which took place shortly before polling day. This provision against the use of oaths and fetishes must surely be unique in plebiscite legislation. In this case the accused was held guilty of announcing that anyone who voted for the first alternative would be bitten by a snake and killed by a fetish known as Atando. The fetish priest was interviewed by the regional officer and agreed to call on the accused to revoke the fetish oath which he had been found guilty of swearing. The accused, however, refused to obey the summons of the priest and was reported to have notified his intention of appealing against his conviction. The leader of the party supporting the first alternative requested the Administrator to disallow any voting in the wards affected. The Administrator replied that he had not power to act in the manner requested and expressed hope that the efforts being made to revoke the fetish would prove successful. He added that a petition could be lodged if this should be considered advisable after examining the results of the voting. When the boxes from one of the villages concerned was opened it was found to contain (besides ballot papers) three or four pieces of paper bearing some legend such as "Please, I am afraid to vote because of the oath sworn by T.A." The percentage of those registered who voted in the two wards affected was 82 per cent and 93 per cent respectively. Eighty votes were cast for the first alternative and 402 for the second. The area was regarded as a place where the party favouring separation would be likely to have a considerable majority. A reasonable inference is that the fetish had only a negligible effect, if any, on the voting." Report of the Plebiscite Administrator on the plebiscite held in Togoland under British administration on 9 May 1956. New York: United Nations, T/1269, p. 5.

[21]Southern Rhodesia Elections, p. 41.

[22]Southern Rhodesia Elections, p. 28.

[23]Southern Rhodesia Elections, p. 6. Neutral observers can use the mass media to good effect: "The Visiting Mission expressed its views in radio broadcasts on three occasions: on the day of its arrival in Palau District, in order to explain the reason for its presence and its role; shortly before the referendum, in order to remind listeners of the most important rules of procedure, especially those relating to the secrecy of the ballot and the freedom of voters to express their views on their future without apprehension of any kind; and lastly, the day following the voting, to call on both sides to respect

the will of the people, whatever it might be, as expressed through universal suffrage." Report of the United Nations Visiting Mission to Observe the Referendum in the Trust Territory of the Pacific Islands, 1978. New York: United Nations, T/1795, p. 38.

[24]Uganda Elections, p. 1.37.

[25]Gregory, p. 89.

[26]Geoffrey Hand, Jacques Georgel, and Christoph Sasse (eds.), European Electoral Systems Handbook (London: Butterworths, 1979), p. 107.

[27]Wambaugh, Saar, p. 252.

[28]Wambaugh, Saar, pp. 252-253.

[29]Gregory, p. 67.

[30]Wambaugh, Plebiscites, p. 246.

[31]Wambaugh, Plebiscites, p. 296.

[32]Southern Rhodesia Elections, p. 57. A similar problem developed at the 1978 referendum in the Trust Territory of the Pacific Islands: "The negatives used in printing the referendum ballot papers in Guam were inadvertently sent to Palau with the ballot papers for that district. In order to prevent any falsification or illegal reproduction, the Visiting Mission suggested that the original (matrix) and the two copies of the original ballot should be kept in a safe place. The Administration agreed that the proposal was well founded and immediately put it into effect on 10 July 1978." Report of the United Nations Visiting Mission to Observe the Referendum in the Trust Territory of the Pacific Islands, 1978. New York: United Nations, T/1795, p. 38.

[33]Southern Rhodesia Elections, p. 57.

[34]Southern Rhodesia Elections, p. 64.

[35]Uganda Elections, p. 26.

[36]Report of the United Nations Visiting Mission to Observe the Referendum in the Trust Territory of the Pacific Islands, 1978, T/1795, p. 46.

[37]Southern Rhodesia Elections, pp. 263-264.

[38]In the 1956 Togoland Plebiscite: "An important innovation was the preparation of reports which the polling agents were invited to sign on the conclusion of their duties. They could either affirm their satisfaction on the conduct of the plebiscite or, alternatively, give particulars of any errors or irregularities which had occurred." Report of the Plebiscite Administrator on the plebiscite held in Togoland under British administration on 9 May 1956. New York: United Nations, T/1269, p. 4. In the Marshall Islands referendum: "At each polling place, each of the opposing parties was authorized to

appoint a representative to observe the voting process. At their first meeting with the Visiting Mission, at Majuro on 26 February, the representatives of The Voice of the Marshalls, the opposition party, pointed out that at the time of the 1978 referendum, the observers from the majority party had received compensation whereas those from The Voice of the Marshalls had not been paid because the party lacked the necessary financial resources. That situation was unfair and prejudicial to The Voice of the Marshalls. The representative of the party added that unless the financial difficulty could be satisfactorily overcome, they would not provide observers on polling day.

"The Mission regarded the problem as very serious and drew the attention of the Election Commissioner to the need to find a solution which would enable observers from both parties to the present. The Election Commissioner decided, in order to place the two sides on an equal footing, to provide identical compensation to all observers, the funds to be taken from the district's operating budget." Report of the United Nations Visiting Mission to Observe the Referendum in the Marshall Islands, Trust Territory of the Pacific Islands, March 1979. New York: United Nations, T/1805, pp. 38-39.

[39] Uganda Elections, p. 8.1.

[40] Wambaugh, Saar, p. 300.

[41] The mixing of ballots is essential when there are small voting localities. See the Report of the United Nations Visiting Mission to Observe the Referendum in the Trust Territory of the Pacific Islands, 1978, T/1795, p. 57.

[42] Report of the United Nations Visiting Mission to Observe the Referendum in the Trust Territory of the Pacific Islands, 1978, T/1795, p. 53.

5

Issues After the Vote

Following the successful conduct of the plebiscite vote, the Plebiscite Commission must study the patterns of voting and issue a recommendation to the Plebiscite Conference. The wide range of potential outcomes to a plebiscite has been discussed earlier--outcomes such as partition between neighboring states, a partition involving the creation of one or more new states, condominium arrangements, etc. While some controversy may develop over the "real" meaning of the vote, the mandate of the voters is usually sufficiently clear to give substance to the recommendation of the Plebiscite Commission. It should be remembered that a plebiscite is an "issue"--not a "candidate"--election and thereby may produce a mandate of considerable clarity.

The Plebiscite Conference must reconvene and pronounce its verdict upon the recommendation of the Commission. Then, together with the Commission, the prescribed outcome must be put into effect.

TRANSFER OF ADMINISTRATION

High-level consultations are required to establish a timetable for the transference of administration from the Plebiscite Commission to the state or states that will take over the plebiscite zone. When the recipient is a well established neighboring state, the transition can usually be brought off in short order. In the 1935 Saar plebiscite the vote was held in early January and the transfer was completed on March 1. Transfer may prove difficult when the recipient is a new state brought into being as a result of the plebiscite vote.

The main issues to be resolved in transfer discussions are (1) monetary and currency questions, (2) compensation for immovable state property, e.g., mines, railroads, (3) treatment of the assets of people leaving the zone, (4) liabilities for social insurance and pensions, (5) the rights of local officials, (6) the new customs regime and border stations, (7) a reassertion of guarantees against reprisals, (8) guarantees for those opting to leave the zone (within a time limit), (9) disposition of the Plebiscite Commission's assets, (10) a schedule for the withdrawal of neutral troops and the introduction of troops of the receiving states. Alternatively, permanent demilitarization of the zone--with inspection--could be considered. Finally, (11) the continuing authority of the Plebiscite Court for a period of at least one year should be finalized.[1]

The key to the sorting-out of these issues is prior agreement--agreement at the Plebiscite Conference preceding the plebiscite. The more detailed the preparatory agreements before the plebiscite, the smoother the transition phase after the plebiscite.

A generous infusion of foreign aid can serve to grease the wheels of transition. Aid can be especially helpful in those areas of local administration that tend to be the hardest hit by changes in sovereignty: transport, education, health, and jail administration.[2]

All in all, the transfer negotiations following a plebiscite tend to go quite smoothly. This is so primarily because the receiving states are the "winners" of the plebiscite and are thus in an affable mood. A generosity may be shown to the "losers" (if any) that would have been unthinkable prior to the plebiscite.

POPULATION TRANSFER

An important protection for the people of a plebiscite zone is the option to emigrate following the vote. If the settlement established by a plebiscite is to bring a lasting peace, members of minority groups finding themselves on the "wrong side" of the new borders must be helped to relocate. The _jus emigrandi_ for religious dissenters has an honored tradition dating back to the Peace of Augsburg (1555) and the Treaty of Westphalia (1648).[3] Population transfer is never a happy expedient. Yet it is an application to the individual of what the plebiscite is to groups: the right to choose the sovereignty under which one lives. Thus, no plebiscite is complete unless due regard is shown to the option to emigrate.

The right to choose emigration following a peaceful settlement of a sovereignty dispute must be assured through the creation of adequate procedures. Rules must be established governing the sale of the immovable property and the sale or transportation out of the zone of the movable belongings of the emigrants. As was done in India and Pakistan in 1947, "referees" may be appointed to supervise and assist those choosing to leave.[4] It is important that the emigrants be assured (1) that they will receive fair market value for property left behind, (2) that ample time be allowed for the sale of said property (to avoid a momentary flooding of the market), (3) that all movable property and assets may be taken out of the zone free of tax or duty (and taken in to the receiving states without tax or duty), and (4) that suitable arrangements be made to receive and resettle them in the states of their choice.

Such free and orderly transfers of population--unlike the forced and chaotic transfers between India and Pakistan--tend to operate smoothly. The state that loses people in the process is often happy to see them go. The state receiving them often feels an obligation to assist fellow nationals. Some eight thousand residents of the Saar--including some eight hundred refugees from Germany who had been living in the Saar--departed the zone, most for France. Abiding by the agreements reached before the German take-over of the Saar, Hitler permitted the orderly departure of these people--many of them Jews--and took steps to insure that all were able to take their property with them.[5]

VIABILITY OF SMALL STATES

Until the middle of the twentieth century one of the strongest arguments used against the aspirations of separatist movements was that of viability. First, it was argued, a state had to be economically viable, that is, it had to have the land, labor, capital, and managerial skill to be economically independent and self-sufficient. Without economic viability a state would be a pawn, a beggar-state contributing only instability to the state system. Second, a state had to be viable in political and security terms. It must have the strength, it was argued, to mount a sufficiently credible defense of its territory so as not to be regarded as "easy pickings" by aggressive neighbors. Of course, the nineteenth and early twentieth century European statesmen who held these views did not apply them to existing small states in Europe--states created or permitted to exist that served useful roles as neutrals or as buffers. Nevertheless, smallness was held in contempt equally by citizens of large states and by citizens of the many small principalities of central and southern Europe. Indeed, the Germans and Italians, long victims of fragmented smallness, were among the most vociferously disdainful of small states. In words which, mutatis mutandis, could have been spoken by British, French, Spanish, or Russian empire-builders (or by those disdainful or micro-states today), Hitler, speaking of Austria, declared in 1938:

> What, what can words like "independence" or "sovereignty" mean for a state of only six millions? . . . To-day it is only under quite peculiar presuppositions that such small state formations can have a possibility of life . . . Even the German Reich is too small; it needs a complement of colonies: how should a state which was but the size of a single province succeed?[6]

The question of viability looks quite different from the perspective of small nations wishing statehood. From their perspective, size alone is not decisive. There are large states in economic shambles and small states with vibrant, self-sufficient economies. In any event, the economic viability argument appears not to deter separatist movements: they simply presume that with statehood will come the power to build a strong economy. Indeed, many view the viability argument as a form of discrimination by the rich against the poor and the large against the small whereby the small poor are denied the power to emerge from their poverty.

The creation of dozens of small states has changed attitudes toward economic viability. Any application of the concept has been official proscribed by the United Nations General Assembly in regard to the Trust Territories, e.g., "the adequacy of political, economic, social or educational preparedness should never serve as a pretext for delaying independence."[7]

The experience of the small states of Western Europe

has undermined the argument that small states cannot be viable in terms of external security. Small countries such as Luxembourg, Belgium, the Netherlands, and Denmark have found a home within the NATO alliance while Switzerland, Sweden,and Yugoslavia have established themselves as neutrals. It is true that the stable alignment of states in Europe is not matched in Africa and Asia. Nevertheless, small nations seeking independence are unlikely to be deterred by viability arguments. Those engaged in armed struggle quickly point to the historic success of the Swiss and the recent success of the Yugoslavs in maintaining an armed neutrality.

In a sense the dire predictions of the nineteenth and early twentieth century statesmen have come true: There are indeed scores of virtual beggar states. Subject to the manipulation of global and regional powers, they are a continuing source of instability. This is all the more so because dissident national groups within these states--believing that independence will cure their own people's economic woes--frequently receive the backing of outside powers.

Now that the era of European or "external" colonialism is drawing to a close, the use of the viability argument as a weapon against seccessionist groups is coming back into vogue. The over one hundred new states--many facing worrisome economic and security problems themselves--are in no mood to grant self-determination to dissident nations within their borders. This is especially so in cases such as Croatia in Yugoslavia and Shaba Province in Zaire where the secessionist area is also the most prosperous area of the existing state. Hence, warnings of "balkanization" are coming from states that did not exist when the term came into use a century ago. Writing about the politics of the Treaty of Versailles (1919), Harold Butler pondered the use of the term.

> It was easy enough to condemn the peace settlement as the "balkanisation of Europe" from arm chairs in London. It was all very well for the economists to demonstrate by industrial and banking statistics that the new grouping of the states was unworkable, and to a large extent they were right. But national sentiment takes little account of statistics. To the traveller who witnessed the ecstasy with which all the liberated peoples were revelling in their newly

> won freedom, it was obvious that the peace settlement was in its broad lines not only right but inevitable.[8]

WHY PLEBISCITES FAIL

Plebiscites, when conducted, rarely fail. The leap of faith that is needed to attempt a plebiscite tends to become the will to implement the result. Several attempts to hold plebiscites have been aborted because of the inability of the plebiscite regime to establish the necessary peaceful, plebiscitary atmosphere. Typical was the case of Teschen, Spisz, and Orava (1920) where the Plebiscite Commission was unable to neutralize the plebiscite zone. The Plebiscite Conference--that of the victorious Allied and Associated Powers--was unwilling to back-up the Commission's efforts to obtain the cooperation of Poland and Czechoslovakia.[9] Provided with too small a staff and too few neutral troops, the Commission was unable to deal with politically-inspired strikes, acts of violence and intimidation, and the meddling of the Polish and Czech governments. The plebiscite was cancelled by mutual agreement.

The attempted plebiscite in Vilna (1920-21) also failed because the key parties were unwilling to permit the neutralization and pacification of the zone. The attempted plebiscite in Tacna and Arica (1925-26) failed because the Plebiscite Commission was not even granted the power to neutralize--or in any way supervise--the local Chilean administration.

The underlying reason for each of the above failures was the fact that key parties to the plebiscite were not "on board" from the very beginning. Poland, Czechoslovakia, and Lithuania were newly constituted states struggling to establish themselves. Their new governments were often internally divided over the handling of the plebiscites. In the case of Poland, the government seemed unable to control certain military units and to keep Polish nationalist agitators from the Vilna plebiscite zone. In Tacna and Arica the plebiscite was the product of an arbitration decision. Thus, the two parties, Chile and Peru, were never in direct agreement. Chile, which had controlled the zone for several decades, saw the plebiscite simply as a legal frosting to cover the cake of annexation. Peru saw it quite differently.

Most aborted plebiscites have been followed by

settlements achieved through direct negotiations. The prospect of a plebiscite seems to concentrate marvelously the minds of statesmen. Deals are often struck that balance the hopes of those who believe they would surely have been "winners" in a plebiscite against the fears of those who saw themselves as likely "losers." As with other forms of peaceful settlement, the plebiscite seems all the more attractive when compared to the grim and costly alternative of war.

NOTES

[1]Satya M. Rai, Partition of the Punjab (Bombay: Asia Publishing House, 1965), pp. 90-120. League of Nations, Ten Years of World Co-operation (Geneva: Secretariat of the League of Nations, 1930), p. 3; 28-29; 74-77. Sarah Wambaugh, The Saar Plebiscite (Cambridge: Harvard University Press, 1940), pp. 309-312.

[2]Rai, p. 97.

[3]Johannes Mattern, The Employment of the Plebiscite in the Determination of Sovereignty (Baltimore: The Johns Hopkins Press, 1920), p. 163.

[4]Rai, pp. 72-145.

[5]George Scott, The Rise and Fall of the League of Nations (London: Hutchinson & Company, 1973), p. 300. Also see Wambaugh, Saar, p. 309.

[6]Quoted in Alfred Cobban, The Nation-State and National Self-Determination (New York: Thomas Y. Crowell, Revised Edition, 1969), p. 20.

[7]United Nations Monthly Chronicle, Vol. X, No. 4 (Apr. 1973), p. 65.

[8]Quoted in Cobban, p. 21.

[9]Sarah Wambaugh, Plebiscites Since the World War (Washington, D.C.: Carnegie Endowment for International Peace, 1933), p. 161.

6

Conclusion

> Democracy is not the problem--elections are the problem.
>
> --Anwar Sadat

Unlike the threat of nuclear holocaust, there is nothing potential about the crisis of illegitimate sovereignty. Millions have been and are being killed. The flood of modern weapons flowing to every corner of the planet insures that those movements fighting for "justice" and those governments fighting for "order" will likely find neither justice nor order. The battles fought within states afflicted with illegitimate sovereignty spillover into other states in the form of assassinations, hijackings, and bombings. Just as Bosnians and Serbians, Sudeten and Danzig Germans provided the ready tinder for World Wars One and Two, so too may obscure peoples and places provide the spark for World War Three.

The issue is this: What is the appropriate role for outsiders? What are the appropriate and effective means for outside states and organizations to participate in the peaceful resolution of sovereignty crises? (Outsiders will participate. The normal operating procedure for such participation is distinctly warlike. States--even international organizations--"play favorites," i.e., provide either the government or rebel faction with weapons, financial aid, and diplomatic backing.) This author suggests three basic ways that outsiders can participate in an appropriate and peaceful manner:

(1) Make manifest to all parties the extraordinary human cost of secessionist, irredentist, and national liberation wars. Such wars are the great killers of our age--either directly through bloodshed or indirectly through hunger or

disease stemming from such wars. It is only a matter of time until the use of nuclear weapons by rebel groups or by beleagered states raises the potential cost to the level of catastrophe.

(2) Make clear to the combatants the alternatives to violence. War is not the only solvent. Most political power does not come "out of the barrel of a gun." Stability and prosperity thrive on consent, agreement, and compromise. Rich and peaceful societies are rich and peaceful to no small extent because they have established legitimate political institutions that command the voluntary loyalty and support of their peoples.

(3) Make available peaceful, impartial mechanisms for legitimate self-determination. Neutral states and international organizations should stand ready to provide the expertise and the resources for the conduct of plebiscites and the supervision of domestic elections. The question is whether the gunman and the bomber will be the agents of change or whether peaceful participatory mechanisms will carry us into the future.

There is no prospect that states will stop "playing favorites." Varying definitions of strategic and economic interest will lead inevitably to support for ruling or insurgent groups. Thus, most states will no doubt continue to view the crisis of illegitimate sovereignty as a matter of "backing the right horse" or at least of raising the cost to the enemy so as to encourage a "deal." Of course, this approach serves only to heap additional fuel on the fires of war and this is candidly recognized by many statesmen who participate in the game. As long as the battles are fought in someone else's homeland and as long as the costs to the patron states are held to modest levels, the game will continue. Given mankind's past and present behavior, few can contest the thesis that violent change will continue to predominate leading, perhaps, to the ultimate ruin of our species.

What has changed in recent years is the spread of the battle zone to the streets, offices, airports—even the embassies—of the patron states. There has also been a sharp rise in the cost of staying in the game. Television has raised the domestic political cost (in liberal democracies) of patronizing small wars around the world. The rapidly increasing sophistication of the weapons used by all sides in separatist and national liberation struggles has made the financial cost of participation unpleasantly high. Worse still, patron states are increasingly vulnerable to being embarrassed by their client states when the clients massacre and brutalize civilians, invade neighboring states, or supplement their incomes by growing and selling narcotics. The eagerness to patronize factions in the "brushfire" wars of the 1950s and 1960s has given way to a sober counting of the costs. The prospect of "losing" a country or a part of a country to the camp of one's enemy is still sufficiently worrisome in domestic political terms for global and regional powers to justify major involvement. However, given the rising costs of military solutions, the threat of military escalation, and of major power involvement, peaceful solutions look increasingly attractive.

THE THEORY OF THE JUST WAR

The twentieth century, the first century to produce over 100 million combat related deaths, has seen a renewed interest by many people in the "Theory of the Just War." In his definitive statement of the theory, St. Thomas Aquinas posits three conditions for a just war: (1) Lawful Authority, (2) Just Cause, and (3) Right Intention.

(1) Lawful Authority

The making of war, according to St. Thomas, "is not the business of a private individual" but the prerogative solely of those in sovereign authority. He cites the reasoning of St. Augustine:

> The natural order conducive to peace among mortals demands that the power to declare and counsel war should be in the hands of those who hold supreme authority.[1]

Thus, only the legitimate holders of authority may prosecute warfare. In our age the holders of authority acquire their license to act from the will of the populace. Consequently, any war which claims to be "popular" may claim, *ipso facto*, to possess lawful authority. Just war theorists have long recognized that non-state groups may launch lawful wars, e.g., underground resistance groups in countries that have been overrun by enemies and whose governments have surrendered. Hence, nearly all national liberation movements, in the eyes of their supporters, easily pass the test of lawful authority.

(2) Just Cause

There must be valid reasons for resort to war. Valid reasons such as the violation of territory and harm to one's population are necessary but not sufficient to justify the taking-up of arms. Three tests must be applied to such valid reasons: (a) Sufficient Proportion, (b) Last Resort, and (c) Fair Hope of Success.

(a) Sufficient Proportion. There must be sufficient proportion between the good to be achieved by fighting and the objective evils inflicted upon the participants in war. As war becomes more and more devastating to the material and moral condition of man, the good to be achieved must be increasingly widespread and profound. In our age only such goods as "independence," "self-determination," and "human rights" are of such overriding value that they outweigh the catastrophic evils of war.

(b) Last Resort. All peaceful means must be exhausted--and be seen to be exhausted--before war may be initiated. Only by attempting all the available peaceful means--means such as negotiation, mediation, arbitration, adjudication, plebiscite, economic sanctions--can proof of the unavoidability of war be established. (There may be risks and costs in first attempting resolution through peaceful means. Such risks and costs must be accepted--they do not justify a short-cut to war.) In our era of instantaneous communication, high speed transport, and high explosive weapons, there is an enormous temptation to "steal a march" on one's opponent through the early initiation of hostilities. Thus, war--the great solvent, the righter of wrongs--is often near the top of the list of options rather than at the bottom.

(c) Fair Hope of Success. There must be a reasonable hope that the war will succeed. If there is little or no hope of success, the war will inflict only evil and achieve little or none of the good that is necessary to give sufficient proportion to the war. Thus, the Theory of the Just War may require surrender or submission when the cause is hopeless. However, our century has witnessed countless examples of "hopeless causes" blossoming into successful new states. The utter improbability of the State of Israel and of several dozen other small states fans the fire of hope for liberation movements everywhere.

(3) Right Intention

Even when lawful authority and just cause are

present, a war may be unjust if those who prosecute it are guided by evil motives. According to St. Thomas:

> Thirdly, it is necessary that the belligerents should have a rightful intention, so that they intend the advancement of the good, or the avoidance of evil. Hence Augustine says: True religion looks upon as peaceful those wars that are waged not for motives of aggrandizement or cruelty, but with the object of securing peace, of punishing evil-doers, and of uplifting the good. For it may happen that the war is declared by the legitimate authority, and for a just cause, and yet be rendered unlawful through a wicked intention. Hence Augustine says: The passion for inflicting harm, the cruel thirst for vengeance, an unpacific and relentless spirit, the fever of revolt, the lust for power, and suchlike things, all these are rightly condemned in war.[2]

Our era is blessed (cursed) with a plenitude of laudable motives for war: freedom, justice, independence, self-determination, territorial integrity, national interest, class struggle, etc.

It is the tragedy of our age that the Theory of the Just War appears to legitimize both wars of "liberation" and the wars waged by states to suppress "liberation" movements. Most claims of lawful authority and right intention are all but unimpeachable in the minds of whose who make the claims. It is in the area of just cause, especially in the prerequisites of sufficient proportion and last resort, that those seeking peaceful resolution can apply moral leverage. The disproportionate damage produced by most civil wars may dampen the fervor of all but the fanatics and the vengeance seekers. The fulcrum, however, is the requirement that force must be the last resort. In the domestic law of most countries all of the available peaceful remedies must be attempted before the plea of "self-defense" may be accepted. At the most basic level, civil order rests upon the principle of last resort. If even a shred of international order is to be achieved, the global community must provide the mechanisms for peaceful resolution--mechanisms such as mediation, arbitration, adjudication, and plebiscite.

COMING TO TERMS WITH THE STATE SYSTEM

Contemporary man continues to indulge the state. States can and do engage in the most heinous atrocities against their own and other peoples. Yet few question the sovereign prerogatives of states that make such conduct possible--even inevitable. States are permitted to build weapons that can destroy much of mankind. We may dislike these weapons but few question the sovereign right of states to build and deploy them. Non-state actors rarely receive such indulgence.

Flora Lewis, in a column entitled "Terrorists Should Find No Indulgence," argues the case against non-state actors:

> Too many observers have succumbed to the temptation to denounce the terrorist deed and sympathize with its purpose . . .
>
> What group will be next to demand "understanding" and political support in return for restraint from wanton killing? The world is full of people who are suffering, let alone of people whose forebears suffered.
>
> A firm line must be drawn. Terrorism cannot work as moral blackmail any more than as political blackmail. Condemnation must be unqualified. Understanding should be reserved for victims. Civilized countries cannot afford to waffle.
>
> History cannot be undone or avenged.[3]

History, of course, is the story of the undoing of history. The future will surely undo the present. In any event, should states which engage in terrorism ("war" or "covert operations") and which routinely engage in blackmail ("deterrence") find no indulgence as well? Would a world in which no state was at war with any other state but in which states killed millions of their domestic dissidents every year be a world at peace?

The state system is an irremovable part of our reality. No alternative system of organizing the world into political entities is anywhere in sight. The issue is not the existence of the state system but of the need for flexibility and adaptability in the system. States, despite their rhetoric, have never been immutable. New states have been hived-off from old ones. Old states have been dissolved and replaced by successor states. Many states today are the product of struggles for self-determination--a concept all but unimagined at the time of Westphalia (1648).

State sovereignty has always been more mystique than fact. Few states have been genuinely sovereign in terms of the Westphalian principles of independence, equality, and unanimity. The authors of the Westphalian formula never dreamed that states would elevate themselves to the status of deities--above law and morality. Natural law and God's law were deemed applicable to all human beings and to all organizations created by human beings. Thus, the idea that states exist under law and should be held accountable for their behavior is not new. In our century, and for the foreseeable future, it is the people's will that holds states to account--if anyone holds states to account. The issue is one of congruence--congruence between the popular will and the configuration of political entities. Political entities can be neatly defined through charters and constitutions. It is the definition and measurement of the popular will that poses the problem. Elections, of course, are the principal means by which this congruence may be established. Political legitimacy arises from the people's will--it does not descend deductively from the Westphalian principles of state sovereignty.

Politicians and statesmen are understandably reluctant to measure the peoples' will too closely or too often. They risk the rejection of themselves and of their policies. Yet it is this willingness to risk rejection that distinguishes the liberal democracies from the dictatorships of the world But even in liberal democracies the rejection of the state itself is regarded as treasonous. It is rare that statesmen provide an electoral mechanism that permits the citizenry to alter the sovereignty under which they live. It usually requires the dislocation of war to force statesmen into organizing plebiscites.

THE IMPARTIALITY OF INTERNATIONAL ORGANIZATIONS

International organizations can encourage the use of the plebiscite in several ways. (1) They can use their good offices to encourage and facilitate the bargaining process which may lead to peaceful resolution--the plebiscite being one mode of peaceful resolution. (2) International organizations can provide useful expertise and experienced personnel. For instance, the United Nations Trusteeship Council has overseen the conduct of over a dozen plebiscites and referenda in the Trust Territories. The Commonwealth has provided Observer Groups to witness elections in several countries in recent years. (3) International organizations can provide the mechanism for the creation of peacekeeping and monitoring forces.

However, international organizations can play these constructive roles only if they are regarded by the parties to a dispute as reasonably impartial. International organizations, like states, may be tempted to "play favorites" in disputes--even to the extent of taking sides with economic and military support. A clear illustration of partiality can be seen in the United Nations General Assembly decision to recognize the South-West Africa People's Organization (SWAPO) as "the sole and authentic" representative of the Namibian (South-West African) people. The merits of the case aside, the United Nations' stance is a pre-judgment of the "will of the people" of Namibia. This pre-judgment raises serious doubts about the ability of the United Nations to supervise impartially an election in Namibia. The South Africans, among others, fear a "napoleonic plebiscite" in which a United Nations-supervised election would clothe the nakedness of a direct hand-over of power to SWAPO.

In his 1982 annual report Secretary-General Javier Perez de Cuellar expressed the fear that the United Nations was becoming a "white elephant" in the vital area of the settlement of international disputes.[4] He noted that in only one dispute (out of over two dozen festering disputes) had the United Nations' efforts brought any visible progress: Namibia. Of course, the United Nations itself, having taken sides in the dispute, was all but paralyzed. The job of impartial conciliation was being done by the five state "Contact Group" acting on behalf of the United Nations. The moral of the story is that impartial international organizations can be found--or created--that can play a constructive role in the business of conflict resolution. Regional international organizations or even <u>ad hoc</u> organizations such as the "Contact Group" can readily fill the void.

THE TASK AHEAD

Liberal democracies have been and remain today the pioneers of democratic technology. They continue to develop and refine measurement techniques whereby the popular will can be reliably and validly assessed. Some of this technology may well be rooted in the political cultures of certain liberal democracies. However, some of this democratic technology may by culture-free--much as assembly-line and computer technologies are readily transferable to many cultures. The techniques of election management developed in the liberal democracies have begun to take root in many corners of the world during the course of this century. (Bureaucratic and police techniques--the technology of state control--have spread and taken deep root already.) The greatest growing consumer demand of our age--the need to participate meaningfully in civic affairs--can be satisfied by the spread of these technologies. Through these technologies peoples and government, consent and authority are brought together in mutually supportive harmony. In the words of Lord Soames:

> In this way the scope of the wilful and the arbitrary, which is always a factor in human destinies, may be reduced; and time--that essential element of all politics--may be afforded to those who must learn new ways. In this manner the people may be carried with their government. . .
>
> For, concealed within the forms and even the aridities of constitutional behaviour there is a subtle healing art--an art which closes wounds, which unites what has been divided, which subdues antagonisms, and which brings people together.[5]

NOTES

[1]Quoted in Austin Fagothey, Right and Reason (St. Louis: C.V. Mosby Company, 1963), p. 454.

[2]Fagothey, p. 454.

[3]Flora Lewis, "Terrorists Should Find No Indulgence," International Herald Tribune, 6-7 August 1983, p. 4.

[4]"South West," South African Digest, 17 September

1982, p. 21.

[5]Lord Soames, "From Rhodesia to Zimbabwe," International Affairs, Vol. 56, No. 3 (Summer 1980), p. 419.

Bibliography

The plebiscite lies at the point where state and nation, war and peace, democratic theory and institutional practice come together. Thus, the relevant literature is vast and varied--evidence of the seamless fabric of political reality. This bibliography is meant as a practical guide for those who in the future seek to research, organize and conduct plebiscites.

Abi-Saab, Georges (1972) "Wars of National Liberation and the Laws of War," Annales d'Etudes Internationales 3, pp. 93-117.

Akzin, Benjamin (1964) State and Nation. London: Hutchinson.

Alexander, Yonah and Robert A. Friedlander (1980) Self-Determination: National, Regional, and Global Dimensions. Boulder: Westview Press.

Alger, Chadwick F. (1961) "Non-Resolution Consequences on the United Nations and Their Effect on International Conflict," Journal of Conflict Resolution 5, pp. 128-222.

Ambedkar, B.R. (1946) Pakistan; Or, The Partition of India, 3rd Edition. London: Thacker.

Andrews, J.A. (1978) "Concept of Statehood and the Acquisition of Territory in the 19th Century," Law Quarterly Review 94, (June), pp. 408-427.

Arrow, Kenneth (1951) Social Choice and Individual Values. New York: John Wiley and Sons.

Baker, Ross K. (1968) "The Emergence of Biafra: Balkanization or Nation-Building," Orbis 12, Spring 1968.

Barros, James (ed.) (1972) The UN: Past, Present and Future. New York: Free Press.

Barth, F. (ed.) (1969) Ethnic Groups and Boundaries. Boston: Little, Brown and Company.

Bassett, John Spencer (1928) The League of Nations: A Chapter in World Politics. New York: Longmans.

Begin, Menachem (1951) The Revolt. New York: Henry Schuman.

Bell, W. and E. Freeman (eds.) (1972) Ethnicity and Nation-Building. Beverly Hills: Sage.

Bendix, R. (1969) Nation-Building and Citizenship. New York: Wiley.

Benello, C. George and Dimitrios Roussopoulos (eds.) (1971) The Case for Participatory Democracy. New York: Grossman.

Benes, Edouard (1971) Bohemia's Case for Independence. London: Allen & Unwin.

Bertelsen, Judy S. (ed.) (1977) Nonstate Nations in International Politics: Comparative System Analyses. New York: Praeger.

Bhutto, Z.A. (1969) The Myth of Independence. London: Oxford University Press.

Bibo, Istvan (1976) The Paralysis of International Institutions and the Remedies. London: The Harvester Press.

Bin Mohamad, Mahathir (1970) The Malay Dilemma. Singapore: Asia Pacific Press.

Bisschop, W.R. (1924) The Saar Controversy. London: Sweet and Maxwell.

Blagoyevitch, V. (1922) Le principe des nationalites et son application dans les traites de paix de Versailles et de Saint-Germain. Paris: Vie Universitaire.

Bloom, S.F. (1941) The World of Nations. New York: Columbia University Press.

Bloomfield, Valerie (1974) "African Elections: Elections Held in Commonwealth Countries of Africa, 1945-1970, A Bibliography and Chronology," Africa Research and Documentation 4, pp. 7-16.

Bogdanor, Vernon (1981) The People and the Party System: The Referendum and Electoral Reform in British Politics. Cambridge: Cambridge University Press.

Bos, Maarten (1968) "Self-Determination by the Grace of History," Netherlands International Law Review 15, pp. 362-373.

Bozeman, Adda (1976) Conflict in Africa: Concepts and Realities. Princeton: Princeton University Press.

Brand, J. (1978) The National Movement in Scotland. London: Routledge.

Breytenbach, Willie J. (1978) "The Salience of African Ethno-Cultural Pluralism with Regard to Democratic Conflict Resolution and Intergroup Accommodation." Paper prepared for the Conference on Southern African Affairs, Institute for Plural Societies, Pretoria University, New York, 23-25 October.

Buchanan, James M. and Gordon Tullock (1962) The Calculus of Consent. Ann Arbor: The University of Michigan Press.

Buchheit, L.C. (1978) Secession. New Haven: Yale University Press.

Bull, Hedley (1971) "Civil Violence and International Order," Adelphi Papers No. 83, Part II, pp. 27-36.

Bull, Hedley (1977) The Anarchical Society: A Study of Order in World Politics. London: Macmillan.

Burgess, E. (1978) "The Resurgence of Ethnicity," Ethnic and Racial Studies 1/3, pp. 265-285.

Butler, David and Austin Ranney (eds.) (1978) Referendums: A Comparative Study of Practice and Theory. Washington, D.C.: American Enterprise Institute for Public Policy Research.

Butler, David and Howard R. Penniman, Austin Ranney (eds.) (1981) Democracy at the Polls: A Comparative Study of Competitive National Elections. Washington, D.C.: American Enterprise Institute for Public Policy Research.

Buxton, Noel and T.P. Conwil-Evans (1922) Oppressed Peoples and the League of Nations. London: Dent.

Byrd, Robert (1963) "Characteristics of Candidates for Election in a Country Approaching Independence: The Case of Uganda," Midwest Journal of Political Science, Vol. 7, No. 1 (February), pp. 1-27.

Cabranes, Jose A. (1975) Self-Determination for Puerto Rico. Washington, D.C.: Office of the Commonwealth of Puerto Rico.

Cahm, E. and V.C. Fisera (eds.) (1978) Socialism and Nationalism. Nottingham: Spokesman.

Calvert, Peter (1982) The Falklands Crisis: The Rights and the Wrongs. London: Frances Pinter Ltd.

Calvert, Peter (1983) Revolution and International Politics. London: Frances Pinter Ltd.

Cameron, David (1974) Nationalism, Self-Determination, and the Quebec Question. Toronto: Macmillan of Canada.

Carr, Edward Hallett (1942) Conditions of Peace. New York: Macmillan.

Carstairs, Andrew McLaren (1980) A Short History of Electoral Systems in Western Europe. London: Allen & Unwin.
Chazan, Naomi (1979) "African Voters at the Polls: A Re-Examination of the Role of Elections in African Politics," Journal of Commonwealth and Comparative Politics 17, pp. 136-158.
Choudhury, G.W. (1975) The Last Days of United Pakistan. Bloomington, Ind.: Indiana University Press.
Chowdhury, S.R. (1977) "Status and Norms of Self-Determination in Contemporary International Law," Netherlands International Law Review 24, pp. 72-91.
Claude, Jr., Inis L. (1955) National Minorities: An International Problem. Cambridge: Harvard University Press.
Claude, Jr., Inis L. (1966) "Collective Legitimization as a Political Function of the UN," International Organization 20, No. 3 (Summer), pp. 367-379.
Cobban, Alfred (1969) The Nation-State and National Self-Determination. Revised Edition. New York: Thomas Y. Crowell.
Coker, Christopher (1981) "Peacekeeping in Southern Africa: The United Nations and Namibia," Journal of Commonwealth and Comparative Politics 19, (July), pp. 319-355.
Connor, W. (1978) "A Nation is a Nation, is a State, is an Ethnic Group, is a . . .," Ethnic and Racial Studies 1/4, pp. 377-400.
Conquest, Robert (1967) Soviet Nationalities Policies in Practice. New York: Praeger.
Cornford, James (1975) The Failure of the State. London: Croom Helm.
Crawford, James (1979) The Creation of States in International Law. Oxford: Clarendon Press.
Crozier, Brian (1960 The Rebels: A Study of Post-War Insurrections. London: Chatto & Windus.
Currie, David P. (1964) Federalism and the New Nations of Africa. Chicago: University of Chicago Press.
Dahl, Robert A. (1956) A Preface to Democratic Theory. Chicago: University of Chicago Press.
Dahl, Robert A. and Edward R. Tufte (1973) Size and Democracy. Stanford: Stanford University Press.
Dale, Richard (1975) "The Glass Palace War or the International Decolonization of Namibia," International Organization 29, No. 2 (Spring), pp. 535-544.

De Jouvenel, Bertrand (1955) De la Souverainete. Paris: Genin.

d'Encausse, Helene Carrere (1979) Decline of an Empire: The Soviet Socialist Republics in Revolt. New York: Newsweek Books.

Denitch, B. (ed.) (1979), Legitimation of Regimes: International Frameworks for Analysis. London: Sage.

Denquin, Jean-Marie (1976) Referendum et Plebiscite. Paris: Librairie generale de droit et de jurisprudence.

De Paos, Liam (1970) Divided Ulster. Baltimore: Penguin Books.

Deutsch, Karl W. (1953) Nationalism and Social Communication. New York: John Wiley & Sons.

Deutsch, Karl W. and Richard Merritt (1970) Nationalism and National Development: An Interdisciplinary Bibliography. Cambridge: MIT Press.

Dinstein, Yoram (1976) "Collective Human Rights of Peoples and Minorities," International and Comparative Law Quarterly 25, pp. 102-120.

Downs, Anthony (1957) An Economic Theory of Democracy. New York: Harper and Brothers.

Dreyer, June T. (1976) China's Forty Millions. Cambridge: Harvard University Press.

Duchacek, Ivo D. (1970) Comparative Federalism: The Territorial Dimension. New York: Holt, Rinehart and Winston.

Duparc, J. Fouques (1922) La protection des minorites de race, de langue, de religion. Paris: Dalloz.

Duverger, Maurice (1951) "The Influence of Electoral Systems on Political Life," International Social Science Bulletin 3, pp. 314-352.

Eagleton, Clyde (1953) "Self-Determination in the United Nations," American Journal of International Law 47, pp. 88-93.

Earle, Valerie (ed.) (1968) Federalism: Infinite Variety in Theory and Practice. Itasca: F.E. Peacock Publishers.

Eckstein, Harry (ed.) (1964) Internal War: Problem and Approaches. New York: Free Press of Glencoe.

Eggleston, Elizabeth M. (1970) "Prospects for United Nations Protection of the Human Rights of Indigenous Minorities," Australian Yearbook of International Law, pp. 68-74.

Eisenstadt, S.N. and Stein Rokkan (eds.) (1973) Building States and Nations. Beverly Hills: Sage Publications, 2 vols.

Emerson, Rupert (1962) From Empire to Nation: The Rise to Self-Assertion of Asian and African Peoples. Cambridge: Harvard University Press.

Emerson, Rupert (1964) Self-Determination Revisited in the Era of Decolonization. Occasional Papers in International Affairs, Harvard University, No. 9, December 1964.

Enloe, Cynthia H. (1973) Ethnic Conflict and Political Development. Boston: Little, Brown and Company.

Eppstein, John (1929) Ten Years' Life of the League of Nations. London: May Fair Press.

Esman, Milton J. (ed.) (1977), Ethnic Conflict in the Western World. Ithaca: Cornell University Press.

Falk, Richard (1968) Legal Order in a Violent World. Princeton: Princeton University Press.

Farley, Lawrence T. (1982) Change Processes in International Organizations. Cambridge: Schenkman Publishing Company.

Finger, Seymour Maxwell (1972) "A New Approach to Colonial Problems at the United Nations," International Organization 26, pp. 143-153.

Forsyth, Murray (1982) "Sovereignty and Confederation: Some Reflections." Paper prepared for the Annual Conference of the British International Studies Association, Southampton, 16-17 December.

Forsyth, Murray (1981) Unions of States: The Theory and Practice of Confederations. Leicester: Leicester University Press.

Franck, Thomas M. (ed.) (1968), Why Federations Fail: An Inquiry into the Requisites for Successful Federalism. New York: New York University Press.

Franck, Thomas M. (1976) "The Stealing of the Sahara," American Journal of International Law 70, pp. 694-721.

Franck, Thomas M. and Paul Hoffman (1976) "The Right of Self-Determination in Very Small Places," New York University Journal of International Law and Politics 8, pp. 331-386.

Friedlander, Robert A. (1977) "Proposed Criteria for Testing the Validity of Self-Determination as It Applies to Disaffected Minorities," Chitty's Law Journal 25, pp. 335-338.

Friedrich, Carl J. (1968) Trends of Federalism in Theory and Practice. New York: Praeger.

Geertz, Clifford (ed.) (1963), Old Societies and New States: The Quest for Modernity in Asia and Africa. New York: The Free Press.

Goldhagen, E. (ed.) (1968) Ethnic Minorities in the Soviet Union. New York: Praeger.

Gooch, G.P. (1920) Nationalism. New York: Harcourt Brace.

Goodhart, Philip (1971) Referendum. London: Tom Stacey, Ltd.

Gordon, David C. (1971) Self-Determination and History in the Third World. Princeton: Princeton University Press.

Gotlieb, Yosef (1982) Self-Determination in the Middle East. New York: Praeger.

Gregory, Martyn (1980) "The Zimbabwe Elections: The Military and Political Aspects," Journal of Southern African Studies 7, pp. 17-37.

Gregory, Martyn (1981) "Zimbabwe 1980: Politicisation through Armed Struggle and Electoral Mobilisation," Journal of Commonwealth and Comparative Politics 19, pp. 62-94.

Gunter, Michael M. (1977) "What Happened to the United Nations Ministate Problem?" American Journal of International Law 71, pp. 110-124.

Gurr, Robert Ted (1970) Why Men Rebel. Princeton: Princeton University Press.

Haas, E.B. (1964) Beyond the Nation State. Stanford: Stanford University Press.

Habermas, J. (1976) Legitimation Crisis. London: Heinemann.

Hachey, Thomas E. (1972) The Problem of Partition: Peril to World Peace. Chicago: Rand McNally.

Hall, Raymond L. (ed.) (1979) Ethnic Autonomy: Comparative Dynamics. New York: Pergamon.

Hand, Geoffrey, et al (eds.) (1979) European Electoral Systems Handbook. London: Butterworths.

Hanna, Willard (1965) The Separation of Singapore from Malaysia. New York: American Universities Field Staff.

Hay, Peter (1966) Federalism and Supranational Organizations: Patterns for New Legal Structures. Urbana: University of Illinois Press.

Hayes, Carlton J. (1937) Historical Evolution of Modern Nationalism. New York: Crowell-Collier-Macmillan.

Hayes, Carlton J. (1963) Nationalism: A Religion. New York: Atherton Press.

Hechter, M. (1975) Internal Colonialism: The Celtic Fringe in British National Development, 1536-1966. London: Routledge and Kegan Paul.

Henderson, William (1975) West New Guinea: The Dispute and Its Settlement. South Orange: Seton Hall University Press.

Hermet, Guy, Richard Rose and Alain Rouquie (eds.) (1978) Elections Without Choice. New York: John Wiley & Sons.

Horowitz, Donald (1971) "Three Dimensions of Ethnic Politics," World Politics 23, January.

Horowitz, Irving Louis (1976) Genocide: State Power and Mass Murder. New Brunswick: Transaction Books.

Howard, John R. (ed.) (1970) Awakening Minorities. Chicago: Aldine.

Hughes, Christopher (1963) Confederacies. Leicester: Leicester University Press.

Ijalaye, D. (1971) "Was Biafra at Any Time a State in International Law?" American Journal of International Law 65, pp. 551-559.

Ikle, Fred C. (1971) Every War Must End. New York: Columbia University Press.

Jacobson, Harold K. (1962) "The United Nations and Colonialism: A Tentative Appraisal," International Organization 16, No. 1 (Winter), pp. 37-56.

James, Alan (1969) The Politics of Peacekeeping. London: Institute for Strategic Studies.

James, Alan (1982) "Sovereignty: Ground Rule or Gibberish." Paper prepared for the Annual Conference of the British International Studies Association, Southampton, 16-17 December.

Jenkins, Brian (1975) International Terrorism: A New Mode of Conflict. Los Angeles: Crescent Publications.

Johnson, C. Don (1973) "Toward Self-Determination - A Reappraisal as Reflected in the Declaration on Friendly Relations," Georgia Journal of International and Comparative Law 3, pp. 145-163.

Johnson, Harold S. (1967) Self-Determination within the Community of Nations. Leyden: Sijthoff.

Johnston, Ray Edward (ed.) (1976) The Politics of Division, Partition, and Unification. New York: Praeger.

Kay, David A. (1972) "The UN and Decolonization," in James Barros (ed.) The UN: Past, Present and Future. New York: Free Press.

Keohane, Robert O. and Joseph S. Nye (eds.) (1970) Transnational Relations and World Politics. Cambridge: Harvard University Press.

Kohn, Hans (1955) Nationalism: Its Meaning and History. Princeton: Van Nostrand.

Kohr, Leopold (1957) The Breakdown of Nations. New York: Rinehart.

Korbel, Josef (1954) Danger in Kashmir. Princeton: Princeton University Press.

Kuper, Leo and M.G. Smith (1969) Pluralism in Africa. Berkeley: University of California Press.

Lakeman, Enid and James D. Lambert (1955) Voting in Democracies. London: Faber and Faber.

Lambert, Richard D. (ed.) (1977) Ethnic Conflict in the World Today. Philadelphia: Annals of the American Academy of Political and Social Science, Vol. 433.

LaPonce, J.A. (1957) "The Protection of Minorities by the Electoral System," Western Political Quarterly 10, pp. 318-339.

League of Nations (1930) Ten Years of World Co-operation. Geneva: Secretariat of the League of Nations.

LeBon, Gustave (1899) The Psychology of Peoples. London: Unwin.

Lendvai, Paul (1969) Eagles in Cobwebs: Nationalism and Communism in the Balkans. New York: Anchor Books.

Lenin, V.I. (1973) The Right of Nations to Self-Determination. Moscow: Progress Publishers.

Levine, Isaac Don (1919) The Resurrected Nations. New York: Stokes.

Lijphart, Arend (1977) Democracy in Plural Societies: A Comparative Exploration. New Haven: Yale University Press.

Linz, Juan J. (1978) The Breakdown of Democratic Regimes: Crisis, Breakdown, and Reequilibration. Baltimore: The Johns Hopkins University Press.

Lissitzyn, Oliver J. (1970) "Territorial Entities other than Independent States in the Law of Treaties," Academie de Droit International, Recueil des Coups 1968. Leyden: Sijthoff, Vol. III, p. 9.

Liston, Robert A. (1977) Terrorism. Nashville: Thomas Nelson.

Livingston, Marius H., et al (1978) International Terrorism in the Contemporary World. Westport: Greenwood.

Livingston, William S. (ed.) (1963) Federalism in the Commonwealth. London: Cassell.

Loescher, Gilburt D. and John A. Scanlon (eds.) (1983) "The Global Refugee Problem: U.S. and World Response," The Annals of the American Academy of Political and Social Science, Vol. 467.

Luard, Evan (1966) The Evolution of International Organizations. London: Thames and Hudson.

Luard, Evan (ed.) (1972) The International Regulation of Civil Wars. New York: New York University Press.

Lubasz, H. (ed.) (1964) The Development of the Modern State. London: Macmillan.

Luce, E.P. (1958) Le referendum du Togo. Paris: Editions Pedone.

Lucien-Brun, J. (1923) Le probleme des minorities devant le droit international. Paris: Spes.

Mackenzie, W.J.M. (1958) Free Elections. London: George Allen and Unwin.

Mackenzie, W.J.M. and Kenneth Robinson (1960) Five Elections in Africa. Oxford: Clarendon Press.

Mackie, Thomas T. and Richard Rose (1982) The International Almanac of Electoral History, 2nd Edition. New York: Facts on File.

McLaurin, R.D. (ed.) (1979) The Political Role of Minority Groups in the Middle East. New York: Praeger Special Studies.

McRoberts, K. (1979) "Internal Colonialism: The Case of Quebec," Ethnic and Racial Studies 2/3, pp. 293-318.

McWhinney, Edward (1966) Federal Constitution Making for a Multinational World. Leyden: Sitjhoff.

Mair, L.P. (1928) The Protection of Minorities: The Working and Scope of the Minorities Treaties under the League of Nations. London: Christophers.

Mankekar, D.R. (1971) Pakistan Colonialism in East Pakistan. Bombay: Somaiya Publishers.

Mansergh, Nicholas (1976) The Prelude to Partition: Concepts and Aims in Ireland and India. Cambridge: Cambridge University Press.

Marshall, Charles Burton (1965) The Exercise of Sovereignty. Baltimore: Johns Hopkins Press.

Mattern, Johannes (1920) The Employment of the Plebiscite in the Determination of Sovereignty. Baltimore: The Johns Hopkins Press.

The Meaning of Intimidation (1980) Salisbury: Catholic Commission for Justice and Peace in Rhodesia.

Merle, M. (1961) "Les Plebiscites Organises Par Les Nations Unies," Annuaire Francaise de Droit International, Vol. 7, pp. 425-445.

Miller, J.B.D. (1981) The World of States. London: Croom Helm.
Milner, Henry and Sheilagh Milner (1973) The Decolonization of Quebec. Toronto: McClelland and Stewart.
Milnor, A.J. (1969) Elections and Political Stability. Boston: Little, Brown.
Moore, John Norton (1969) "The Control of Foreign Intervention in International Affairs," Virginia Journal of International Law 9, pp. 209-342.
Morgan, E. and R. Vineberg (1978) "Elections in Africa: A Select Bibliography," Occasional Papers No. 14, The Harry S. Truman Research Institute, The Hebrew University of Jerusalem.
Morris-Jones, W.H. (ed.) (1981) From Rhodesia to Zimbabwe: Behind and Beyond Lancaster House. London: Frank Cass and Co.
Mulford, David C. (1964) The Northern Rhodesia General Election 1962. Nairobi: Oxford University Press.
Murray, J.N. (1957) The UN Trusteeship System. Urbana: University of Illinois Press.
Mustafa, Zubeida (1971) "The Principle of Self-Determination in International Law," International Lawyer 5, pp. 479-487.
Nairn, T. (1977) The Break-Up of Britain. London: New Left Books.
Nanda, Ved P. (1972) "A Critique of the United Nations Inaction in the Bangladesh Crisis," Denver Law Journal 49, pp. 53-67.
Neuberger, B. (1976) "The African Concept of Balkanisation," Journal of Modern African Studies 13, pp. 523-529.
Nicholls, David (1975) The Pluralist State. London: The Macmillan Press Ltd.
The 1980 Rhodesian Elections: A Report (1980) Salisbury: Catholic Institute for International Relations.
Nordlinger, Eric A. (1972) Conflict Regulation in Divided Societies. Cambridge: Center for International Affairs, Harvard University, C.F.I.A. Occasional Paper No. 29.
Northedge, F.S. (1976) The International Political System. London: Faber.
Ofuatey-Kodjoe, W. (1977) The Principle of Self-Determination in International Law. New York: Nellen Publishing Co.

Olorunsola, V. (ed.) (1972) The Politics of Cultural Subnationalism in Africa. New York: Anchor Books.

Osborne, Sidney (1921) The Problem of Upper Silesia. London: Allen Unwin.

Osborne, Sidney (1923) The Saar Question. London: Allen Unwin.

Paine, Lauran (1975) The Terrorists. London: Hale.

Palley, C. (1979) The Rhodesian Election. London: Catholic Institute for International Relations.

Palloni, A. (1979) "Internal Colonialism or Clientelistic Politics? The Case of Southern Italy," Ethnic and Racial Studies 2/3, pp. 360-377.

Panter-Brick, S.K. (1968) "The Right to Self-Determination: Its Application to Nigeria." International Affairs 44, April.

Papadopoulos, Andrestinos N. (1982) Multilateral Diplomacy within the Commonwealth. The Hague: Martinus Nijhoff.

Parry, Albert (1976) Terrorism: From Robespierre to Arafat. New York: Vanguard.

Patterson, Orlando (1977) Ethnic Chauvinism: The Reactionary Impulse. New York: Stein and Day.

Payne, S. (1971) "Catalan and Basque Nationalism," Journal of Contemporary History 6/1, pp. 15-51.

Penniman, Howard R. (1967) Decision in South Vietnam. Washington, D.C.: The Free Society Association, Inc.

Penniman, Howard R. (1972) Elections in South Vietnam. Washington, D.C.: American Enterprise Institute for Public Policy Research.

Pennock, J. Roland (1979) Democratic Political Theory. Princeton: Princeton University Press.

Pillsbury, W.B. (1919) The Psychology of Nationality and Internationalism. New York: Appleton.

The Plebiscite on the Political Status of Puerto Rico (1967) Department of State of Puerto Rico, Overseas Information Service, San Juan, Puerto Rico.

Pomerance, Michla (1974) "Methods of Self-Determination and the Argument of 'Primitiveness,'" Canadian Yearbook of International Law: 1974 12, pp. 38-66.

Pomerance, Michla (1982) Self-Determination in Law and Practice. The Hague: Martinus Nijhoff.

Poggi, G. (1978) The Development of the Modern State. London: Hutchinson and Co.

Popper, F. (1971) "Internal War as a Stimulant to Political Development," Comparative Political Studies 3, pp. 413-423.

Priou, J. (1923) Le Territoire du Sarre. Paris: Berger-Levrault.

Provizer, Norman W. (1977) "The National Electoral Process and State Building: Proposals for New Methods of Elections in Uganda," Comparative Politics 9, No. 3 (April), pp. 305-326.

Rae, Douglas (1967) The Political Consequences of Electoral Laws. New Haven: Yale University Press.

Rai, Satya M. (1965) Partition of the Punjab. Bombay: Asia Publishing House.

Rajan, M.S. (1961) The United Nations and Domestic Jurisdiction. New York: Asia Publishing House.

Rakowska-Harmstone, Teresa (1970) Russia and Nationalism in Central Asia: The Case of Tadzhikistan. Baltimore: The Johns Hopkins University Press.

Randle, Robert F. (1973) The Origins of Peace. New York: The Free Press.

Ratnam, K.J. and R.S. Milne (1967) The Malayan Parliamentary Election of 1964. Singapore: University of Malaya Press.

Reece, J. (1979) "Internal Colonialism: The Case of Brittany," Ethnic and Racial Studies 2/3, pp. 275-292.

Reid, George L. (1974) "The Impact of Very Small Size on the International Behavior of Microstates," Sage Professional Papers in International Studies 2, 02-027.

Rejai, Mostafa and Cynthia H. Enloe (1969) "Nation-States and State-Nations," International Studies Quarterly 13, pp. 140-158.

The Report of the Commonwealth Observer Group on Elections Leading to Independent Zimbabwe (1980) London: Commonwealth Secretariat.

Rigo Sureda, A. (1973) The Evolution of the Right to Self-Determination: A Study of United Nations Practice. Leiden: A.W. Sijthoff.

Rivlin, Benjamin (1955) "Self-Determination and Dependent Areas," International Conciliation, No. 501, January.

Rokkan, Stein (1970) Citizens, Elections, Parties. Oslo: Universitetsforlaget.

Rokkan, Stein and Derek W. Urwin (eds.) (1982) The Politics of Territorial Identity. London: Sage Publications.

Ronen, D. (1979) The Quest for Self-Determination. New Haven: Yale University Press.

Rose, Richard and Harve H. Mossawir, Jr. (1967) "Voting and Elections: A Functional Analysis," Political Studies 15, No. 2 (June), pp. 173-201.

Rose, Richard (1979) "Ungovernability: Is There Fire Behind the Smoke?" Political Studies 17, No. 3 (September), pp. 351-370.

Rosenau, James N. (ed.) (1964) International Aspects of Civil Strife. Princeton: Princeton University Press.

Rotberg, R. (1967) "African Nationalism: Concept or Confusion?" Journal of Modern African Studies 4, pp. 33-46.

Rothschild, Donald S. (1961) "The Politics of African Separatism." Journal of International Affairs 15.

Russell, Bertrand (1917) Why Men Fight. New York: Century.

Ryan, William (1970) Blaming the Victim. New York: Pantheon.

Prefaces to Peace: A Symposium (1943) with Wendell L. Wilkie, Herbert Hoover, Henry A. Wallace, Sumner Wells, etc. New York: Simon and Schuster.

Sartre, Jean Paul (1968) On Genocide. Boston: Beacon Press.

Savigear, Peter (1983) "Corsica: Regional Autonomy or Violence," Conflict Studies (London), No. 149.

Sayre, F.B. (1919) Experiments in International Administration. New York: Harper.

Schermerhorn, R. (1970) Comparative Ethnic Relations. New York: Random House.

Schermerhorn, R. (1978) Ethnic Plurality in India. Tucson: University of Arizona Press.

Schoenberg, Harris O. (1976) "Limits of Self-Determination," Israel Yearbook on Human Rights, pp. 91-103.

Schreuder, D.M. (1980) The Scramble for Africa, 1877-1895: The Politics of Partition Reappraised. Cambridge: Cambridge University Press.

Schwebel, Stephen M. (1974) "Wars of Liberation - As Fought in U.N. Organs," in John Norton Moore (ed.) Law and Civil War in the Modern World. Baltimore and London: Johns Hopkins University Press, pp. 446-457.

Schweigler, G. (1975) National Consciousness in Divided Germany. Farnborough: Saxon House.

Scott, George (1973) The Rise and Fall of the League of Nations. London: Hutchinson & Company.

Seton-Watson, H. (1977) Nations and States. London: Methuen.

Shaheen, S. (1956) The Communist Theory of Self-Determination. The Hague: Van Hoeve.

Sharpe, L.J. (ed.) (1979), Decentralist Trends in Western Democracies. London: Sage.

Sicard, G. (1964) "Referendums et plebiscites dans l'histoire de France," Revue des sciences politiques (February-March), pp. 85-116.

Simmonds, G.W. (ed.) (1977), Nationalism in the USSR and Eastern Europe in the Era of Brezhnev and Kosygin. Detroit: University of Detroit Press.

Smith, Anthony D. (1979) Nationalism in the Twentieth Century. Oxford: Martin Robertson.

Smith, Anthony D. (1981) The Ethnic Revival. Cambridge: Cambridge University Press.

Smith, Gordon (1976) "The Functional Properties of the Referendum," European Journal of Political Research 4, pp. 1-23.

Smith, T.E. (1960) Elections in Developing Countries. London: Macmillan.

Snyder, Louis L. (1968) The Meaning of Nationalism. New York: Greenwood Press.

Soja, Edward W., (1971), The Political Organization of Space. Washington, D.C.: Association of American Geographers, Resource Paper No. 8.

Southall, R.J. (1972) Parties and Politics in Bunyoro. Kampala: Makerere Institute of Social Research.

Stalin, J. (1936) Marxism and the National Self-Determination in Soviet Foreign Policy. Moscow: Foreign Language Publishing House.

Stone, J. (1979) "Introduction: Internal Colonialism in Comparative Perspective," Ethnic and Racial Studies 2/3, pp. 255-259.

Suhrke, Astri and Lela Garner Noble (eds.) (1977) Ethnic Conflict in International Relations. New York: Praeger.

Suzuki, Eisuke (1976) "Self-Determination and World Public Order: Community Response to Territorial Separation," Virginia Journal of International Law 16, pp. 779-862.

Tarrow, Sidney, et al (eds.) (1978) Territorial Politics in Industrial Nations. New York: Praeger.

Tiewul, S. Azadon (1975) "Relations between the United Nations Organization and the Organization of African Unity in the Settlement of Secessionist Conflicts," Harvard International Law Journal 16, pp. 259-302.

Tilly, C. (ed.) (1975) The Formation of National States in Western Europe. Princeton: Princeton University Press.

Tivey, Leonard (ed.) (1981) The Nation-State: The Formation of Modern Politics. Oxford: Martin Robertson.

Toussaint, Charmian Edwards (1956) The Trusteeship System of the United Nations. London: Stevens & Sons.

Umozurike, U.O. (1972) Self-Determination in International Law. Hamden: Archon.

UNITAR (1971) Small States and Territories: Status and Problems. New York: Arno Press.

Van den Berghe, Pierre L. (1967) Race and Racism: A Comparative Perspective. New York: Wiley.

Van den Berghe, Pierre L. and Paul Brass (1976) "Ethnicity and Nationalism in World Perspective," Ethnicity 3.

van der Merwe, H.W. and R.A. Schrire (1980) Race and Ethnicity in International Perspective. Cape Town: David Philips.

Van Dyke, Vernon (1974) "Human Rights and the Rights of Groups," American Journal of Political Science 18, pp. 725-741.

Van Dyke, Vernon (1977) "The Individual, the State, and Ethnic Communities in Political Theory," World Politics 29, pp. 343-369.

Van Dyke, Vernon (1978) "The Right of a People to Preserve Its Culture." Paper prepared for the Conference on Southern African Affairs, Institute for Plural Societies, Pretoria University, New York, 23-25 October.

Verdery, K. (1979) "Internal Colonialism in Austria-Hungary," Ethnic and Racial Studies 2/3, pp. 378-399.

Volova, L.I. (1972) Plebistsit v Mezhdunarodnom Prave. Moscow: IMO.

Wainhouse, David W. (1964) Remnants of Empire: The United Nations and the End of Colonialism. New York: Harper & Row.

Waldheim, Kurt (1971) The Austrian Example. New York: Macmillan.

Walters, F.P. (1975) A History of the League of Nations. London: Oxford University Press.

Wambaugh, Sarah (1933) Plebiscites Since the World War. Washington, D.C.: Carnegie Endowment for International Peace.

Wambaugh, Sarah (1940) The Saar Plebiscite. Cambridge: Harvard University Press.

Watson, Francis M. (1976) Political Terrorism: The Threat and the Response. New York: Luce.

Weil, Gordon L. (1970) The Benelux Nations: The Politics of Small-Country Democracies. New York: Holt, Rinehart and Winston.

Wiatr, Jerzy J. (1969) Narod i Panstwo: Socjologiczne Aspektry Kwestu Narodowcj (Nation and State: Sociological Aspects of the National Question). Warsaw: Academy of Sciences.

Williams, Colin H. (ed.) (1982) National Separatism. Vancouver and London: University of British Columbia Press.

Wilson, A. Jeyaratnam (1975) Electoral Politics in an Emergent State: The Ceylon General Election of May 1970. London: Cambridge University Press.

Wilson, Joe F. (1979) The United States, Chile and Peru in the Tacna and Arica Plebiscite. Lanham: University Press of America.

Wirsing, Robert G. (ed.) (1981) Protection of Ethnic Minorities: Comparative Perspectives. New York: Pergamon Press.

Wittmann, Erno (1919) Past and Future of the Right of National Self-Determination. Amsterdam: Van Holkema and Warendorf.

Ydit, Meir (1961) Internationalised Territories. Leyden: Sythoff.

Young, Crawford (1976) The Politics of Cultural Pluralism. Madison: University of Wisconsin Press.

Young, Oran R. (1967) The Intermediaries: Third Parties in International Crises. Princeton: Princeton University Press.

Index